Just call me López

Other Books by Margaret Silf

Simple Faith

The Other Side of Chaos

Compass Points

Going on Retreat

Close to the Heart

Inner Compass

Just call me López

Getting to the Heart of Ignatius of Loyola

MARGARET SILF

LOYOLA PRESS.
A JESUIT MINISTRY
Chicago

LOYOLA PRESS.
A JESUIT MINISTRY

3441 N. Ashland Avenue
Chicago, Illinois 60657
(800) 621-1008
www.loyolapress.com

cover photo © Image Source Photography/Veer.
cover illustration © Sterling Hundley

Back End Pages, clockwise from l to r:
(a) © LoyolaPress; (b) © iStockphoto/Thinkstock; (c) © LoyolaPress;
(d) © LoyolaPress; (e) © iStockphoto.com/stevehong; (f) © Sterling Hundley;
(g) © LoyolaPress; (h) © iStockphoto/abzee; (i) © Croberto68/Wikipedia;
(j) © c./Shutterstock; (k) © Photos.com/Getty Images

Library of Congress Cataloging-in-Publication Data
Silf, Margaret.
  Just call me López : getting to the heart of Ignatius Loyola / Margaret Silf.
      p. cm.
  Includes bibliographical references.
  ISBN-13: 978-0-8294-3668-6
  ISBN-10: 0-8294-3668-5
1. Ignatius, of Loyola, Saint, 1491-1556. 2. Christian saints--Spain--Biography.
3. Spiritual life--Catholic Church. 4. Spirituality--Catholic Church. I. Title.
  BX4700.L7S55 2012
  271'.5302—dc23
  [B]

2012013605

Printed in the United States of America.
12 13 14 15 16 17 Bang 10 9 8 7 6 5 4 3 2 1

For López with heartfelt gratitude,
and for all friends of López, past, present, and to come,
especially those who are also friends of mine

Contents

Foreword

I have heard Jesuits nervously joke that they have no fear of coming face-to-face with Almighty God in Heaven, but are filled with trepidation at the prospect of meeting Ignatius of Loyola!

The biographies I've read of Ignatius over the years have done little to diminish his reputation of being somewhat fierce and forbidding. Having said that, I've noted that his contemporaries—the people who actually were with him and worked alongside him—all seemed to love him and to enjoy being with him.

It was with this in mind that I asked Margaret Silf—someone with a profound insight into Ignatian spirituality—to consider writing a short book about Ignatius that wouldn't be simply another biography but would give a twenty-first-century reader insight into this man's humanity. I asked for a telling of his story that would help us better understand what Ignatius's spiritual experiences offer us, even today.

Margaret has written a powerful work of imagination that places us with Rachel, our narrator, in contact with "López" (this is one part of Ignatius's full name) at pivotal moments in his life. We are rooted with Rachel in the present; it is Ignatius who somehow "time shifts" to be with us. This requires some suspension of disbelief, but it is a small price to pay for being allowed to listen to these two spiritual companions who have so much to learn from each other.

Margaret has succeeded not only in showing us Ignatius's warm and compassionate character, but she also introduces us to the important stages in his journey (a timeline is provided at book's end) and gives an excellent outline of his famous "Spiritual Exercises."

I love what Margaret has written here. I hope you do, too.

Paul Brian Campbell, SJ
March, 2012

Preface

$\mathcal{I}$ walked along the beach one morning and noticed something glinting in the sand. When I stooped to pick it up, I had in my hand just a piece of broken glass. I could easily have hurt myself on it, but instead I held it between my fingers and watched as the sun's rays fell upon it. A miracle happened. The invisible light of the sun suddenly became visible in a whole spectrum of color as the light was refracted—bent!—through the broken glass, to create a rainbow.

Miracles so often happen in the midst of brokenness, inadequacy, and failure. In fact, those experiences would seem to be God's preferred location for the work of transformation.

In the conversations that unfold in this book, I would like to invite you to meet, and engage with, one of God's pieces of broken glass. I have called him simply López, which is his middle name. We know him more commonly as Inigo, who later took the name Ignatius of Loyola.

At the beginning of his story, we meet someone who is vain, ambitious, even arrogant, and certainly of dubious moral standing. As he gradually shares his story, we can see the transformative power of grace in action. The man we might dismiss, or even fear, at the beginning of the story, gradually discloses a history of vulnerability and imperfection. The more the vulnerability is revealed and acknowledged, the more the power of divine light increases, penetrating the brokenness to create the rainbow.

When I was first invited to write this story, I refused, on the grounds that I have no experience in writing biography, let alone hagiography. The publishers were insistent. Over an extended breakfast, with a bottomless coffeepot and a visionary editor, in a backstreet Chicago café, I was persuaded. Not to write a biography, but to tell a story.

When I first encountered Ignatius, many years earlier, I guess I would have thought of him as someone I would probably not want to meet in heaven: a soldier, a rather legalistic individual with views of the church that would differ widely from my own, and the founder of a religious order that had the reputation of being the papal shock troops in the war against the Protestant Reformation, a war with which I would have had little sympathy. Under the wise guidance of some of his twentieth-century sons, I saw my view of him move rather toward respect, and even reverence, for someone I had to acknowledge as a saint, certainly someone much more complex than I had imagined, someone who had something important to teach us.

By the time I embarked upon the venture of this book, I realized I had developed a certain guarded affection for him. It was this incipient affection and curiosity as to what it was that made him tick that, along with the breakfast and the coffee and the enthusiastic editor, persuaded me to risk setting out on the journey that these conversations reveal. By the time I came to write the final section, when López leaves for the last time, just as a single star is rising into the night sky, I found myself writing through my tears. I knew then that López had become as much a part of my own life as he had of the narrator's. I think I can honestly say that I have never enjoyed writing a book as much as I have enjoyed this one, or been so deeply moved by any subject as I have been by this. The personal encounter with López has changed me in ways I could never have imagined. My hope is that he will tell you, the reader, his story in ways that might be transformative for you also.

Is this a work of biography or of the imagination? Both, really. The facts about Ignatius's life and person that I have included are biographically accurate. The story of the narrator, as she engages with her unexpected guest, is a work of the imagination. Rachel is not me. Her story is not my story. The interaction between them is God's story, and I hope that, as such, it will speak to *your* story.

Rachel meets López with no preconceived ideas about him. He is a stranger to her, and she does not even share his religious background. Rachel is, perhaps, a postchurch pilgrim, searching for her own deepest truth and struggling with her own life's issues, meeting heart-to-heart with López across the divide of five centuries of history and a huge cultural disconnection. That they relate so deeply with each other across these gulfs is part of the miracle, reflecting the greater miracle that Ignatian spirituality is even more relevant to our world today than it was when he walked the length and breadth of Europe in his pilgrim sandals.

And conversations, of course, were Ignatius's preferred method of engaging with the lives of the people he met. The art of spiritual conversation is one of the most valuable aspects of his legacy to us. The conversation with Rachel would have been, for him, the most natural and obvious "way of proceeding."

Over the course of his life, with all its joys and its despair—its struggles, humiliations, and graces—López is being honed and polished by divine love, from a piece of broken glass into a finely finished prism that we can hold in our hands today, a prism through which the invisible light of God is bent and refracted into the colors of everyday life—our everyday lives.

Enjoy your pilgrimage as you explore, with him and with God, the colors of your own soul's journey—a journey that invites you to grow from bent and broken to translucent and transformed.

Margaret Silf
February 2012

A Story Begins

I never knew what hit me.

One minute I was cycling, somewhat distractedly, along the familiar streets of my hometown. The next minute I was sprawled on the sidewalk, stunned, my cycle a crumpled heap on the roadside. As to the cause of this disruption to the smooth running of things, all I could see of him were his exhaust fumes as he sped away from the scene, leaving not a trace behind except my demolished cycle and the searing pain in my ankle.

The street was deserted. I lay for a while, wondering how to get home. Then the stranger came up to me.

"Can I help?" he asked. "You seem to have run into trouble."

I was speechless with gratitude. My anger with the hit-and-run driver dissolved into pure thankfulness that I was no longer alone with my problem. I looked into the face of my rescuer and saw kindly eyes. Right then, that was all I needed to see. I gratefully accepted his offer to see me back to my home. He picked up the wreckage of the bike in one firm movement and with his free hand supported my arm. Together, we hobbled home.

That's when I became aware that he, too, had a limp. One day I would hear the story behind the limp, but right now I rested my weight on his arm and guided him back to my little apartment, a few blocks away.

"When life knocks you sideways," he said, as we walked, "sometimes it's the beginning of something new, something that takes you completely by surprise."

I paused in my unsteady tracks for a moment and gazed at him. Those words seemed to have come straight from his heart. I found myself curious to know him better. I felt that he knew much more about the mystery of things than he was revealing. I wanted to know what it was that he knew, what dream fired him up, what story underpinned these little glimpses of wisdom he shed upon my plight.

He could not possibly know that my "plight" involved far more than this sudden spill from my bicycle. Or that, at the moment the car struck me, I could hardly see it for all the other scenarios alive in my mind. To say I'd been preoccupied would be an understatement. The accident had merely brought to manifestation the state of my heart that day. No, he couldn't know this, yet he spoke as if he knew that my story was much bigger, much deeper.

By the time we had walked the half mile or so to where I lived, I felt the spirit of a deeper friendship calling us to walk many more miles together. I invited him in for coffee, knowing that this could be an encounter with unpredictable consequences. And he unhesitatingly accepted my invitation. He came in through my door that day, but he brought with him a story that would gradually coax my own story to life.

"You're hurt," he sympathized. But I was already forgetting the pain in my ankle because of the sense of peace I felt in this man's presence.

"I'll survive," I said brightly. *Well, I hope I'll survive,* I thought, in a darker part of myself.

"You will do more than survive," he said. "Our hurts can be the places where we start to grow. One day you may look back with gratitude to the reckless driver who knocked you off your bike."

Who was this stranger, sitting drinking coffee in my home? A short, thin, middle-aged man; not a local man, I felt sure, or I would have recognized him. He looked strangely out of place in the modern world. But there was something timeless in his face.

For a while he sat in silence, but it was a confident kind of silence, as if he were assessing the place and deciding whether he might feel at ease here. I was doing my own assessment, watching his face, noticing the calm surface—the look of self-possession under which, I was sure, lay a story. This man had known turmoil, loss, and disappointment. His life had not been a walk in the park. The eyes that met mine were sharp, clear, and frighteningly perceptive.

"I know this sounds bizarre," he said, finally breaking the pregnant silence. "I actually lived more than five hundred years ago. On my five-hundredth birthday, *you* were in midlife yourself, and going through a time of growth and turmoil, were you not?"

For a moment, I was speechless. There had certainly been serious turmoil in my life over the past twenty years or so, and just a couple of months ago, around the time of my fiftieth birthday, I had received a shocking phone call, and with it some new demands upon my life. Not only that, but my work had just recently become quite interesting, and not in a good way.

"Well," I said with some hesitancy, "I suppose you've got the turmoil right. Only time will tell about the growth."

He smiled. "Now a chance accident has thrown us together. However, I don't think anything happens by chance."

"I don't have any idea who you are," I said, after a bewildered pause, as I tried to make sense of these revelations. "And yet I feel as if I know you. I don't even know your name."

"Just call me López," he replied. He looked at me, eyes raised in question.

"I'm Rachel," I said.

"It's a pleasure to meet you, Rachel. But I must go now. And you must rest."

"I will," I promised.

A slightly awkward silence ensued before both of us simultaneously began to speak.

"Why don't you come and visit again," I began.

"It would be good to continue this conversation," he said at the exact same moment. We laughed at ourselves.

And so it began.

What follows is the story of how it unfolded.

Milk, Fire, and Roasted Chestnuts

We had agreed to meet again. How we had met in the first place I did not understand—and, to be truthful, I had not quite heard what he said about having lived five hundred years before. The rational part of me insisted that this was a metaphor of some sort, and the rest of me refused to linger on the question. As the day approached, I found myself thinking, off and on, about what might lie ahead. I hadn't expected this stranger with his engaging ways and unfathomed depths to preoccupy my thoughts so much. I didn't really know whether I was looking forward to our coming conversation or wishing I had never agreed to this crazy proposition to continue a conversation with a man I did not know.

What, I asked myself, did I most want to ask him? In the end, I decided to let him do most of the talking, given that talking to strangers seemed to be absolutely no problem for him, even if they were five hundred years younger and had a very different world-view. Well, we would see how it went. . . .

The doorbell rang, and I let him in, trying not to let my eagerness—or my anxieties—show too much. He shed his coat in my hallway and made a beeline for the chair he had apparently singled out as his location of choice in my home. The awkward silence I had feared never had opportunity to take hold. After inquiring about the state of my ankle, he plunged his hand into his pocket and pulled out a little paper bag. Pushing it in my direction, he said, "I brought these. Thought you might like to try them. Hope you like them as much as I do."

With unconcealed curiosity I delved into the little bag to find four freshly roasted chestnuts, straight from the brazier! My brain seized up, making me incapable of forming the obvious question: "Where did you get these on a fine sunny evening in the suburbs?"

"This is a special occasion for me," he explained, "a kind of feast day. And it has always been my habit to celebrate feast days by allowing myself this modest treat." His eyes rested on the chestnuts as if they were pure gold. "I'm pleased that we met. I think we have a story to explore together, and I'm glad your ankle is better. Three reasons to celebrate. Now, help yourself, while they are still hot, and I'll tell you how it all began."

He settled back, chestnut in hand. "I was born under a wandering, exciting, adventurous star," he told me. I felt the goose bumps work their way along my arms and neck. "I stumbled into the world at a time of huge transition: the end of the medieval period and the start of the Renaissance. New birth—"

"You really are . . .?" I didn't know how to ask the obvious: *Have you really travelled across time to sit in my living room?*

"The answer is yes," he said, in quite a straightforward way. "It's not important that you understand *how*

I am here but that I *am* here. If I've learned little else about the life of the soul, I do know that appreciating the present moment—whether it's mundane or mysterious—is always the best way to go."

I made a little jump, then, in my mind and heart. I would just accept what was happening. Oddly enough, once I chose to do that, my thoughts were travelling right alongside López's as he picked up his train of thought. "To be born into a time of new birthing brings a certain responsibility, don't you think? It makes you into something of a midwife."

I thought about my own times at the start of the twenty-first century, and it wasn't hard to see the similarities. "We are living through that kind of period now," I suggested. "We're not moving from the medieval to the Renaissance, but the changes are fast and furious, and they leave us breathless—sometimes afraid."

"Exactly!" he said, with unexpected vigor, as though he had been waiting for me finally to make the connection.

And so, as we indulged in our chestnuts, a story began to unfold that spanned the intervening centuries with no sense of dislocation of either time or place.

"Michelangelo was sixteen years older than I, and Martin Luther eight years older," he said. "What a pair of big brothers!" He smiled. "And when I was a year old, Christopher Columbus sailed to the New World, under the flag of Spain, of course."

"And a thousand years after Brendan the Navigator of Ireland made that voyage," I added under my breath, not wanting to take too much wind out of his proud Spanish sails. He ignored my intervention and went on to describe the ferment of excitement that goes with living through an age of discovery, of pushing known boundaries, of risking the great beyond, of relentlessly searching for "more."

"And I had a little sister, too," he said. "Over in Ávila, a little girl called Teresa was born years later. She grew up to make waves in high places! And we are still close." He smiled warmly. "You would love her."

"And your birth family?" I was eager to hear more.

"We were a mixed bunch. I was the last shake of the tree—number thirteen—with eight brothers and four sisters."

"Thirteen," I mused. "Lucky or unlucky?"

He pondered that for a moment. "Both! Unlucky, because my father died when I was still a teenager, and my mother died when I was very young. In fact, I don't remember her, and that makes me very sad. And unlucky because, well," he hesitated. "If I'm honest, I have to admit that we had a pretty dreadful reputation—high beliefs but low standards, you might say. Brawls-on-Saturdays, Mass-on-Sundays, kind of thing. And sometimes worse than brawls. Sometimes serious harm. Not to mention the illegitimate children that have to be counted among our brood."

That last remark delivered a silent shock to my system, deep down. Could he possibly know there was such a child at the edges of my own life? But I responded, "It sounds a lot like today's world." I thought of the volatile mix of unbridled sex and violence alongside the growing longing for spirituality that mark our times. "And what part of your beginning was lucky?"

His face relaxed, and his eyes began to shine. "Well, leaving aside the obvious good fortune of being born into a landed family when there was so much poverty around, I was so lucky to grow up where I did, and surrounded by good folk such as Maria Garin. Maria was a real mother to me. She was my wet nurse, but that was only the beginning of our relationship. As I grew up, I so loved to go and visit her and her family. They were peasant folk, living in the little village of Eguibar not far from our castle. That was my childhood idyll. I close my eyes now, and I can see the bright blue skies over my Basque homeland, the meadows and mountains, the stream flowing through the valley, and there, nestling at the heart of it, the simplicity and warmth of their very ordinary home. I can feel the closeness of Maria as she held me in her arms and told me stories about the creatures all around us, the woods and the pastures, and our Basque history. They loved me as if I were their natural child."

The thought of such love being possible made my eyes misty.

"Maria's husband, Martin de Erratzti, was the local blacksmith, and when I was a child, I loved to stand in the smithy and watch him at work. I delighted in the flames and the sparks, and marveled at how from all the heat and molten metal something hard and durable emerged, something real and solid. He transformed this raw energy into tools that helped people live their lives more fully. I wanted to do that too. He was passionate about his work. I wanted to be that passionate about something."

He glanced up and saw me looking at him intently. I was pretty certain that he did, eventually, live out the sort of passion he spoke of. Apparently reassured that I was not just listening but entering into his story, he continued, "And that was where the chestnuts came in. Maria gathered them, and Martin roasted them, and together we enjoyed them. And today we celebrate again, you and I, because our souls have connected."

His reminiscences seemed to fill the room and bring a beautiful sense of peace and gratitude with them. I felt I was actually there, in that remote valley in the foothills of the Pyrenees, where a little Basque boy first tasted the milk of human kindness, the fire of human passion and creativity—and roasted chestnuts!

2

Illusion, Disillusion

When you engage in a conversation with the past, I guess you should be ready for whatever comes. What came next time, however, found me seriously unprepared. I had, quite reasonably I thought, come to expect my now almost familiar companion, my undersized middle-aged gentleman, limping, and dressed in ways that wouldn't attract undue attention. This I could cope with.

The person who crossed my threshold but a week later was something else altogether. I hesitated momentarily between a powerful desire to keep him at a safe distance and an equally strong urge to get him safely inside before the neighbors noticed him. That this was López was not in doubt; I could see that in his bright eyes and determined brow. But why the flamboyant clothes?

I watched, speechless, as he strutted along my hallway and installed himself in his usual seat. He was decked out in a suit that could have rivaled Joseph's coat of many colors. Tight hosiery and shining boots showed off his short legs, and a wide cape flew open to reveal this feast of color. The cherry on the cake, so to speak, was provided by—get this!—a scarlet cap, topped by a fine flourish of feather waving in the breeze, a dancing complement to his long red-blond, curly hair.

He grinned at me. "I left the arms at the door, as courtesy demands."

And then I noticed the sword and dagger, the breastplate, the mail corselet, and a bow and arrows, neatly stacked inside my front door.

It took me a moment to gather my thoughts. Either this man had indeed materialized from five centuries ago, or he was on his way to a royal wedding. He broke into my astonishment. "If we are going to revisit my life," he said, "I thought we should do it properly, so you could get a feel for how it really was."

Then, "My father wanted me to be a cleric."

"Really!" My tone betrayed my disbelief immediately.

"Yes," he went on. "Being the thirteenth child didn't do much for my options in the career line. He signed me up for the ecclesiastical life when I was very young. I think it was some kind of insurance policy. But fortunately he never took it too seriously.

"Mind you, it came in useful once when I was in trouble with the police in Azpeitia, near our home. My brother (he was the parish priest) and I were often in trouble, womanizing, brawling, and so on, but this time it got serious, and I hightailed it into the bishop's jurisdiction and claimed what you would have to call ecclesiastical immunity. I sure thanked my old dad that day, for his foresight."

"Hmm." My mind was racing. "The more things change, the more they stay the same."

He raised his eyebrows. "How so?"

By way of an answer I pushed across a copy of the latest newspapers. The headlines spelled it out in stark capitals:

SEX SCANDALS COVERED UP BY BISHOPS.

OFFENDERS MOVED ON UNCHALLENGED TO SAFE LOCATIONS.

PRESERVING INSTITUTION MORE IMPORTANT THAN CARING FOR VICTIMS.

He glanced at the papers, first briefly, then with real engagement. He didn't respond. But I noticed that the feather in his cap began to wilt a bit, and the expression on his face deepened from frivolity to concern.

After a short pause while we both reflected on these connections, he resumed his story. "We had a relative in high places, at the court and close to the king, who had once offered to take one of our boys to train as a page. So, number thirteen got the lucky break, and when I was sixteen, I found myself riding south, to the lands of no less a one than Juan Velazquez de Cuellar."

He paused, to see whether this had impressed me, and I noticed his fleeting disappointment. But, undeterred by my lack of enthusiasm, he described how he had embarked on this new stage of his life equipped with little more than a moderate ability to sing and dance and a goodly pedigree. And so, dreaming of fame and glory in the courts of Old Castile, he had bade farewell to family and friends, not least Maria and Martin, and galloped forth into the sunset. I smiled. He was irrepressible.

"And how did it go?" I asked.

"Just great, for quite a while. I learned to speak Castilian, and I quickly picked up the gentler arts of how to behave in court: when to speak and when to be silent, whom to impress and whom to ignore. It was my noviceship for greater things, I hoped, and I gave it my best efforts. I certainly gave Velasquez, and hence the king, my wholehearted loyalty. That was how things were. When the king called, you responded."

"And were these great men worthy of such whole-hearted allegiance, do you think?"

"Nobody would ever have asked such a question," he answered, rather sharply, as though it were impertinent on my part even to suggest the possibility of doubt.

I stuck to my twenty-first-century guns. "But *now*," I insisted. "How would you answer the question now?"

"I guess my dreams of glory were something of an illusion," he admitted. "I have to say that, because suddenly the wind began to blow from a different direction. King Ferdinand died in 1516, and his successor, Charles I, began to put pressure on my employer to give up his lands. Protest was futile. It sobered me up, I can tell you. I realized how uncertain these allegiances are, how they have no real foundation, represent no lasting loyalties. Then Velasquez died, and I was out of a job. I was sent on my way with five hundred escudos and two horses and the suggestion that I should seek out the Duke of Najera. From now on I was going to have to trust my own deeds, my own courage and skill, not the words of others, however high-sounding."

He fell silent then, no doubt remembering his misplaced trust. I was remembering illusions of my own, of people whose loyalty I had trusted, of work that I loved but that increasingly brought me up against resistance, and questions of allegiance and integrity. Such life lessons stretch across the centuries.

"But every cloud has a silver lining." Once again his busy eyes sought out mine. "For me this setback opened up the door to a soldier's career when the Duke of Najera took me on for military training, and perhaps that was closer to what I had always dreamed of. Just look at me! Don't you think I suit the part? Spain is going from strength to strength, and so am I. My country is not just conquering Europe. We are sending our brave conquistadors to the New World—nothing can stop us now! And I am part of it. One day my name will be remembered as a fine and noble servant of the king, helping to spread his kingdom across the globe. Mark my words."

And with a flourish he breezed out the door, feather flying high again.

"But which king?" I was left murmuring to his empty chair. "And whose kingdom?"

3

Shattered

everal weeks passed. I barely noticed, because in spite of recent complications in my work life, I had been very busy that month, and traveling a great deal. When I finally landed at home, a whole new set of flowers had bloomed in my little garden out back.

When López returned, a day or so after I did, it was a very different man who sat crumpled up in my home. I couldn't believe my eyes when he arrived, clearly in pain, and mortified in some deeper way as well.

"For goodness' sake, sit down and rest," I said, gazing at him with real concern. "Whatever happened?"

"My aunt knew," he whispered. "She warned me. She must have seen it coming."

Was he delirious as well as injured? But he went on. "She said to me on one of my visits home, 'You will never learn or become wise until someone breaks your leg.'"

There was a long silence. It looked as if someone had done exactly that. The agony was written all over his face. And gradually, painfully, the story trickled forth.

The call to arms had come suddenly, when Captain Herrera summoned his senior officers to an emergency meeting. The fort of Pamplona stood in disputed territory between France and Spain in the Kingdom of Navarre that, until the Spanish took it over, had been fiercely independent. For now, the Spanish held it and were seen as an occupying force, but the French were advancing in vastly superior numbers. The loyalty of the local people could not be counted on. The fortifications wouldn't withstand too much punishment. There was talk of surrender.

López pulled himself up in the chair. "Surrender?" he almost shouted. "Do I look like someone who surrenders?"

Whatever else I might be thinking about my strange guest, the word *surrender* certainly didn't come to mind. This man might be foolish and conceited, but there was something in him that I was beginning genuinely to admire.

"It looks like you stood your ground," I remarked.

"I stood my ground until my legs were shot away from under me," he boasted, flinching even as he uttered the words. "My aunt would have laughed."

"No," I corrected. "Your aunt would have wept."

He glanced at me, almost as though he had never coupled the two ideas of "courage" and "compassion," had never considered that harsh words of warning can be spoken out of tender love.

"What a failure." He sighed, miserably.

"What a transformation," I suggested.

"Transformation?" An eyebrow shot up. "How do you get transformation out of defeat?"

"Well," I said, choosing my words carefully, "I'm thinking of Martin de Erratzti and his blacksmith's fire. Of how that fierce heat and those flashing flames turn raw metal into durable tools, but only when it has been through the agony of the blacksmith's hammer and the cruel bed of the anvil. I'm thinking you are lying on that cruel bed, right now. Could it possibly be a place of transformation?"

"The only evidence of transformation I was aware of after the cannonball hit me was the transformation from vertical to horizontal," he admitted. "Without warning my world was blown apart. I was used to commanding the situation, being in control, *conquering*. And now the French victors were commanding me, controlling my next move, conquering . . ." he could hardly bear to pronounce the word, ". . . conquering *me*!"

"Is that how it felt?" I encouraged him to keep on exploring this, the greatest trauma life had dealt him so far. Frankly, I was in my element. Helping people tell their stories is what I do for a living.

He gave me a quizzical look, as if to say, "How do you *think* it felt?" But then he became more thoughtful, and he told me how events had unfolded. How he had been left with only minimal medical attention while the ceasefire was negotiated—left to ponder his situation and gulp the air of defeat. How he had felt mortified by his enforced impotence and enraged by those who had fled the scene, as he saw it. I could imagine this courtly young man and fearless soldier with his fine manners and high hopes, literally biting the dust and choking on the fumes of failure.

"They were decent men, though, the French," he added. "Warfare in my day wasn't like it is now. The vanquished enemy was still treated as a human being. The French officers came alongside me where I was—no crowing or gloating. They did their best to help me. And then the final honor, or the ultimate mortification, whichever way you look at it: they carried me home on a stretcher. And that was no easy journey I can tell you, across the rough mountain tracks. It took forever. We had to keep stopping, and I felt every jolt in every bone of my body."

"Where was 'home'?" I asked.

"Well, Velasquez was dead, and there was certainly no future in Pamplona after the defenses fell and the French took over. I had no option but to direct them back to the family castle, though I couldn't imagine how I would be received there. Actually, my sister-in-law, Magdalena, was there for me, and I am so grateful to her for her gentleness and kindness. She cared for me when I was helpless to care for myself. I guess I would never have discovered that depth of kindness if the cannonball hadn't knocked me out. Her love was 'home' to me. But I despised those wretches who had run away when things got hot in Pamplona!"

Then he became deeply serious and sat for a while in a thoughtful silence.

"You know what?" he said finally. "Until that moment when the cannonball, in one fell swoop, shattered my leg and my ambitions, I didn't realize how I had spent my life walking my own path, and actually walking away from God. I had been the center of my own world. I think that was the moment when I caught a glimpse from a very different angle. When you are flattened in defeat, you get to look up, and, just possibly, you might see God looking down on you."

"Looking down," I repeated.

"But looking down with compassion," he added. "I'd never seen that before."

Another long and pregnant silence, then, "Perhaps I'm the one who has been running away all my life. And now I've been carried home, helpless."

4

Close Call

*I*f at our last meeting López had been crushed and crumpled, this time there was a pall of serious disgruntlement over the obvious pain he was still experiencing.

"How's the leg?" I asked, then immediately wondered whether this was such a good subject to broach. I was learning that he could be tetchy when he was in pain or upset, and at present he was clearly both of those things.

"I shouldn't complain," he began, "but, courteous as those French soldiers were, their surgeon wasn't up to much. It turns out he botched my leg when he set it, and it had to be done over again."

Ouch! I thought silently, then added out loud, "That sounds excruciating."

"Well, it certainly wasn't a picnic in the park," he admitted. "It wasn't surgery—it was butchery, but I coped. I can handle pain."

My guess was that he had done more than "cope." He seemed like a man who would do anything to avoid revealing his own pain. The courage he had shown, however misguided, on the parapets at Pamplona, would surely have been reflected in his fortitude under the "butcher's" knife. I didn't need him to remind me that five hundred years ago there would have been no anesthetic and precious little surgical hygiene. I looked again, in awe, at his shattered leg in its bandages. I can hardly cope with a toothache, and here he was, still going strong, still undeterred. The only parts of his anatomy that betrayed the agony he was in were his clenched fists and white knuckles.

My friend was still going strong, but where was he heading, and how would that inner strength find expression as his life moved beyond the defeat of his military dreams?

"Can you believe I made my last confession and nearly made it home to the angels?" He grinned at me with a flicker of amusement.

"Was it that bad?"

"It was the eve of St. Peter's Day, June 28, 1521. I was well and truly on my last one-and-a-half legs and had a raging fever. And through the haze I heard the doctor's verdict: 'If he doesn't improve by midnight, it's the end for him.' Maybe somewhere deep inside, my soul took that as a challenge. Or maybe," he added wryly, "the angels weren't quite ready for me! Either way, the next morning I was through with the fever, and I had turned a corner."

Turned a corner. That sounds so simple, I thought. Across the room, the message light on my phone was blinking madly. More complaints, or more voices of support? Another message I didn't know how to answer? If I was turning a corner, it was more like a very long curve.

I noticed López looking at me intently; he'd caught me with my mind elsewhere. "Are you all right?" he asked, sounding genuinely concerned.

"Yes. I was just thinking about how dramatically things can change. Tell me, did your near-death experience make any difference to how you see things?"

His answer was a resounding silence while he thought about the question. Then, "Let's say it was perhaps the beginning of a journey that would lead to change."

"It's hard that change must be so painful sometimes," I said quietly, looking at his bandages. I really hoped he would say more. I needed to hear more. But I would have to wait for our conversations to deepen further before he shared the true extent of the transformation that had begun with the defeat at Pamplona.

Meanwhile, he was visibly frustrated at the confinement his physical condition imposed upon him. Magdalena must have been quite the ministering angel to her sick and suffering brother-in-law. He had nothing but grateful praise for her. But it was very much the old López who languished in her care—a man whose chief concern was still about how to make an impression on ladies in high places, how to turn heads in the high street. I could not believe what came next!

"It was this lumpy bone sticking out of my leg that still troubled me." He sent a rueful glance in my direction. "How was I ever to look good again in my fine hose and shiny boots? There was only one thing for it. I had to let them try to cut it away. This third effort at hacking my leg into shape was the most painful of all. They filed away the protruding bone and then stretched my leg so that it wouldn't be too much shorter than the other one. But I'm not looking for sympathy."

Which was just as well, because I was rapidly running out of it.

And so the convalescence dragged on, and the convalescent grew more and more disgruntled, this time with the after-effects of his now-cosmetic surgery. Perhaps his aunt had been right. Only she had counted wrong. He wouldn't learn to be wise until someone had broken his leg *three* times.

"If at least they had had some decent reading material on offer," he mumbled.

"That was a problem?" I imagined that a castle would surely have had a well-stocked library.

"It was for *me*. All I wanted was a few *caballerias*," he muttered, petulantly.

"Which are . . .?"

"Well, you know, romances, stories of the valiant deeds of knights, tales of dragons and heroes. They were all the rage then. Anyone who was anyone would have read them." He looked at me with an expression veering between scorn at my ignorance and pity for my obvious lack of taste.

"Sounds like you've been reading too many books," I said, in my own defense. "Maybe you should write one instead."

He looked surprised at that but made no further comment.

"So, what did you settle for?" I asked. It was just a polite question really, the sort you might ask a stranger at a party.

"I settled for what they had," he said with a yawn, "and what they had was—imagine this for a man of my position—a *Life of Christ*, and a book on the lives of the saints—in Castilian."

"Oh dear," I commiserated. But he had dropped off to sleep, and the conversation was over.

❧ 5 ❧

Dreams and Reality

*H*ave you ever been in love?" López started our next conversation brightly. "But of course you have," he added, without waiting for an answer. I wasn't sure I wanted to follow him too far down this route. I was more interested in *his* story, so I left him to draw his own conclusions from my quiet smile, and left the question open for further disclosure on his part, since he seemed to be in the mood for sharing something of his heart's journey.

"The great love of my life was a queen, no less," he announced.

"Of earth or heaven?"

"Now there's a question!" He threw back his head and laughed. "At first, very much a queen of the earth. She was my great dream, the object of all my longings. And what's more, I believed that I could one day capture her heart, when the time was right. One day she would see me and acknowledge me as her chosen one. My dreams kept me going, through all the butchery on my leg. Everything would be worth it, if only she would notice me, beckon me to her side, return my ardor."

I could see that this was going to be one of those evenings! Had my thrice-broken companion regressed to adolescence?

"And how did this paragon become a queen of heaven?" I asked.

"No, it wasn't like that." His tone changed noticeably, and his expression grew suddenly much more mature. "The queen of heaven was quite a different matter." I fixed him with my gaze, willing him to tell me more, sensing somehow that he was on the brink of something very significant.

"I was bored out of my mind," he admitted, "and eventually, in desperation, I reluctantly picked up the books Magdalena had left with me."

I understood completely, being myself a person who will read the telephone directory if nothing else is available.

"In spite of myself, I found myself riveted to them. Here were stories of the great saints—of Francis, and Dominic and Benedict, and all the things they endured for the sake of their dreams. I was inspired in a way I had never expected. And then there was the epic tale of Jesus of Nazareth and his mother, Mary. She became the mother I had never known, the sister-in-law who loved me even more than Magdalena did, the queen for whom I would fight any foe, conquer any hardship. I was falling in love, but this time it was for real."

I hoped there was no hint of cynicism in my smile. I didn't mean for there to be, but maybe he picked up a trace.

"I can imagine how all this sounds," he said. "Just another whim on the part of a rather self-centered young man. But it really was different. You see, these stories were *true*."

"True!" I echoed, with conviction. "And that made all the difference?"

"It wasn't quite so simple," he said. "You see, I was still confined to bed, and locked in the realm of dreams. I wasn't in a position to turn anything into action. So dreaming is what I did. And it was my *dreams* that showed me the difference between truth and fantasy. I made dream sandwiches, you might say. One layer, dreams about my lovely lady and all the valiant deeds I would perform to win her love. And the next layer, dreams about Jesus, Mary, and the saints and how I could, if I chose, spend my life and energy for *them*, give my heart for the vision that fired *them*."

"Sounds like a substantial and rather fiery sandwich," I said. "Didn't it give you indigestion?"

"Not at all. It left me hungering for more. I got to thinking that I could do everything those great saints had done—and more! I had proved my mettle against the French. I could surely stand my ground in the battle for human souls. I knew I wanted to enlist in this heavenly army."

"So the highborn lady was jilted in favor of long-gone saints?"

"No, I didn't banish her from my dreams. But I noticed something interesting. Whenever I indulged in daydreams about my earthly queen, I certainly enjoyed them, and they left me intoxicated, but that feeling didn't last. It was like drinking a flask of fine wine. Nice while it lasts, but the pleasure soon passes. But when I dreamed about outsainting the saints, about following Jesus and revering his mother, it was more like an ongoing infusion of a quite different kind of spirit. And the feeling didn't fade."

"It sounds a bit like the difference between falling in love and actually sustaining a loving relationship," I suggested. "The experts say that the state of being in love lasts on average about eighteen months. Only when it is over does the real loving begin."

This comment seemed to resonate with him. "Yes, that rings true. My fantasies about earthly love and conquest were, basically, insubstantial. They could be shattered by a cannonball or a scornful rejection. My dreams about following another King—well, they had a ring of enduring reality about them."

We sat for a while in the profound silence. I knew that López had moved in a new direction. It was a crazy story, but deeply true. I could tell that he was relating to me a process that had changed his life, and I felt humbled that he had been willing to share it with me.

"Last time we met, you said I should read fewer romances and write a book myself," he said.

"Did I say that? Yes, I suppose so."

"After our conversation that day, I wondered why you suggested that. It's not often a person is encouraged to write books."

"I was thinking more specifically of your writing *your* story," I said. His gaze was still questioning, so I went on. "Actually, I help a lot of people write their stories."

"How so?"

"I'm a teacher of sorts. I help people write their spiritual autobiographies."

"Spiritual autobiography. . . ." He seemed to be trying out the words. Then realization flooded his expression. "Oh! Why, that's a good idea, a very good idea. But—" he slowly pulled a sheaf of papers from his satchel.

"What's that?" He had my interest.

"It's not autobiography . . . well, maybe it is, in a way." He handed me the papers. "These are my meditations on the Gospels."

I leafed through page after page of imaginative reflections on gospel scenes and incidents, beautifully scripted in his practiced hand, the words of Jesus written in red ink, and those of Mary in blue ink.

"López, this most certainly is your story, an important part of it. I'm honored that you would let me read it."

"I'm honored that anyone would want to. It isn't finished, of course."

"No. It's not finished because you're living it," I said. "But I hope you keep writing it as well."

He nodded, grateful for the affirmation. I could tell that many pages would follow.

🦢 6 🦢

Visions, Valedictions

*F*ull of the zeal of one who has discovered a whole new way of seeing things, López almost leaped across my threshold, so eager to tell the next chapter of his story, and flush with the kind of fire that was little short of a burning bush. The energy surge knocked me sideways.

"I'm guessing your dreams are taking flight," I said, by way of greeting. "What's going on?"

"I'm going to Jerusalem," he announced, in a tone that left no room for debate.

"Where did *that* come from?"

He seized upon my invitation to describe all that had been happening since we last met. How he had been using his enforced immobility to read more and more from the once-despised books about Jesus and the stories of the saints, and how all the while his leg had been steadily growing stronger, through nine long months of convalescence.

"Nine months' gestation for this new birth," I commented, and he smiled, appreciating this recognition of the new person he was becoming.

"But not an easy pregnancy," he added. "Once I had begun to realize that my frivolous daydreams left me feeling ultimately flat and dispirited, while my deeper dreams of following Jesus and emulating the saints left me feeling energized, I was confronted by the question, What am I going to do about this?"

"I've been pondering this mystery," he continued. "You remember how we talked about the smithy back home and how Martin turned raw energy and molten metal into tools that people could actually use?"

I nodded.

"Well, I really think this is a kind of tool. If it's true that the dreams and desires that come from God leave us inspired and energized, and the ones that come only from our self-focused thinking leave us ultimately empty and flat, wouldn't that be a way of trying to work out which movements in our hearts are really coming from God and which are not?"

I found excitement rising in me; López was onto something important here. His word "movements" struck me particularly. I asked him to elaborate.

"Perhaps these movements are to do with our moods and feelings," he said.

"Moods? Feelings? Surely we can't trust our own moods and feelings—they change like the weather and are just as unreliable."

"That's right," he agreed. "But they are still the first indicators of what is going on in our hearts. The trick would be to get underneath them and ask what they are really about. So, if I am feeling disgruntled and grouchy, what is the reason? Is it perhaps because the world isn't dancing to my music? I have to admit that a bad mood is a sure sign that something very willful in me is kicking too hard and protesting because things are not going the way I want them to."

"In this century, we call that the ego," I said. "It's that part of the self that tries to be in control of everything and always wants its way."

He laughed. "That sounds a lot like large portions of my life!"

"Everyone struggles with the ego-self; it's part of what we call the human condition."

"But back to the emotions," he said, picking up his train of thought. "If the . . . ego . . . is not kicking so hard, if I'm feeling deep-down peaceful, and at balance, calm and receptive, that tells me that God is at work down there in my heart, maybe urging me to serve others in some way, or confirming a good decision I've made. There's so much more to ponder and work on in this, I know, but this has been my experience over these past months."

"Was there any moment when you really *knew* that this deep change was for real?" I asked.

He hesitated. I felt I had walked onto very sacred ground, and almost wanted to take off my shoes. His eyes were focused on the middle distance, his face serious, but relaxed and at peace.

"Yes," he said, almost reluctantly. "You may think I was imagining this, but one night there *was* such a moment. Just for an instant—a moment out of time—the room seemed to fill with light and what I can describe only as a total sense of well-being. In that light I almost thought I could see Mary holding the child Jesus. The moment passed almost instantly, but I knew it had changed me forever. When you've been touched, even momentarily, by perfect purity, you know that you can never again be content to be impure. Memories of my old life, with its violence and debauchery, its utter worldliness, sickened me to the core. It was as if that moment of pure light had revealed my shadows alarmingly, and all I wanted was to set it all behind me, make amends for my many wrong acts and thoughts, and set my course in a new direction."

After what seemed like a very long and companionable silence between us, he roused himself. "You know, I'm a soldier at heart, maybe always will be. I've seen, all too often, the sight of enemy standards flying, threatening to overwhelm us. I've rallied to the standard of my country, Spain, and committed my total loyalty to that standard. But that night I could see that there was a much bigger battle going on, not for territory, but for hearts and minds. Another King was calling me to arms. Another loyalty, far surpassing my loyalty to my country or my flag, was asking for my allegiance. For all my life so far, I've been throwing my energy into things that did not conform to the standard of this King. In fact I have rallied to the opposite standard—that of the King's enemy. It will take a lifetime to atone for that treachery."

"You can't be a traitor to a King you didn't yet know," I suggested. He appeared unconvinced.

"But now is the time to choose which standard I will follow. For everyone, perhaps, there comes a moment to decide."

"What does this decision mean for you, now?" I asked.

"I have taken leave of my family. It wasn't easy. I told them I was reporting back to my old commanding officer. I didn't mention my real intentions, but they knew I was fundamentally changed. They had already seen the signs, and they tried hard to dissuade me from doing anything they would see as extreme or radical. I know their concerns were about the honor of the family name. Their ideas of honor and mine are drifting apart now, and I couldn't guarantee anything. Everything is in God's hands now."

As he left that evening, I wondered if this had been his last visit. The thought saddened me. For the first time I realized that López was becoming part of my own life. And this went deeper than my usual interest in another's story. I was trained to help people delve into their pasts and to write about them. Usually I arrived in some other city, stayed a few days, taught people a skill, then left to prepare for the next engagement. But López's story was somehow mine now. I had hoped we might go many more miles together along the road of experience, but I would have to be content to let that rest in God's hands too.

7

Spot the Mule

I needn't have worried. López was back, sure enough, and I don't think I had ever seen him really angry before. His eyes flashed alarmingly as he flopped into the comfortable chair and drew breath. What had happened to the calm resolution and sure convictions of the man who had left "for Jerusalem"?

"Let me get you some iced water," I suggested, and then, picking up his baleful look, quickly revised the offer to a cool beer.

"So what's eating you up?" I asked, when he seemed to be a bit calmer. And then the story poured forth, Niagara-style.

He had been making his way quietly along the trail, he said, riding his mule (I wondered briefly whether he had parked the animal in a restricted zone outside my apartment, but then decided to let go of the thought). From his description, it sounded as though he had been lost in holy thoughts and high intentions when the unexpected encounter happened.

I sat up. "An encounter? Please go on." It's my belief that unexpected encounters are a sure sign of a greater mind than ours at work. López continued his story.

Along his peaceful way, he had run into a stranger, a Moor—by definition a Muslim—and therefore likely to hold different views of gods and men than those cherished by López. I wondered how the conversation had gone. He took a deep breath, and already the vapor was starting to rise from his ears again. Their conversation, which may well have begun amicably, had evidently turned sour when the Moor questioned the continuing virginal state of Mary after the birth of Jesus. López, newly recruited into the active Catholic army, was having none of this. For such heresy the man must die, he vowed to himself.

"How did that decision sit with your choice to follow the Prince of Peace?" I asked. I omitted mentioning the matter of turning the other cheek and loving your enemies. I figured he could bring those things to mind for himself.

He swallowed hard. Then, if anything, I can only say he looked a bit sheepish—or even mulish! Eyes lowered, he went on to explain the finer points of how he had discerned whether or not to kill the Moor.

I have to say I was impressed! He had decided that the mule might make a wiser choice than he would himself, given the mood he was in. When they had come to a fork in the road and the Moor had gone off in the direction of his own destination, López had curbed his immediate desire to go after him, and instead had settled the matter thus: if the mule chose the path the Moor had taken, he would pursue him and dispatch him. If the mule chose the other path, he would allow the offender to go free and live. The mule chose the path of peace, and the Moor, presumably, lived to tell the tale.

Yet here was López, still spitting fire over the matter. I wondered what exactly it was that was fueling the flames.

"I guess you think I was overreacting?" He threw a sideways glance in my direction. I wasn't really thinking anything of the sort. In fact, I was casting my eyes over the several dozen books on spiritual discernment adorning my bookshelves, none of which actually mentioned mules.

I tried to put myself in my companion's shoes. I asked myself how I might react to someone who challenges some deeply held belief. Would I make the effort to understand where my challenger was coming from, or would I lash out in anger, as López had been tempted to do?

"I can think of plenty of ways that someone like your Moor might challenge some of *my* entrenched positions," I said, "and I wouldn't like it any more than you did. When you let the mule decide the outcome, I guess you were actually stepping back from the brink, counting to ten, and giving the situation a bit of cool-down time. We know now that our brains work like that. Whenever we are threatened, our 'lower,' primitive brain urges us to fight or escape. But if we can just count to ten, that gives our higher brain a chance to respond and, maybe, to choose a better course than instant retaliation."

My companion seemed to sink a little more comfortably into his chair, mulling over this information.

"Perhaps everyone needs a mule," he said, smiling. "Better yet, perhaps governments should have them! Think of the wars we would be spared if kings and such made decisions out of that higher brain, as you called it.

"Imagine," he went on, "how things might be if *your* leaders took time at the crossroads of every crisis, to let the higher brain decide."

"How true," I interjected. "If we had a few 'mules' that afforded us time to think and willingness to listen to the other side, there would certainly be fewer programs of revenge and preemptive strikes, less playground bickering and politicking and posturing, and some chance of moving on in a constructive way."

"Yes," he said, "they should all listen to my mule and stop at the brink of a situation before stepping over the line. The time it takes to stop and think might be the difference between bad and worse, between manageable tension and irreversible catastrophe."

And this, coming from the man who had wanted to conquer the world, and whose stubbornness at Pamplona had cost him his leg yet had opened the door to a whole new way of being López. God writes straight with crooked lines, and sends asses to teach us to be wise.

"Have you ever had a mule experience?" He asked this innocently enough, looking straight at me. I looked right back, not out of any resolve or argument but because my mind had gone blank. If a mule did show up in my life, what would it look like?

"I know it wouldn't be a real mule," he said, while I poured us another beer. "But as I was telling you about mine, it seemed that a look of recognition crossed your face." My, he was frighteningly observant.

"Well, I can recall a time or two when I really wanted to rush a decision or—oh, here's a mule! Not long ago in fact, I had a tangle with a certain person who had been at one of my presentations. She said something to me that seemed very judgmental and unfair. But when she said it, other people were present and the topic shifted, and I had to leave it. The two of us still needed to work together the following day. So that evening I picked up the phone to call her. I'd been simmering all afternoon, and I knew exactly what to say to set her straight! But only moments after we began the conversation, another call came through, from my brother, and I had to take that call because of a serious situation he was in at the time. So I told the woman we would have to talk later."

"And did you?" He was in rapt attention.

"Yes, but by the next day I'd had second thoughts about my little speech, and our conversation was much more tempered and reasonable. It had been a miscommunication, not an attack on me personally. I was so glad I had been prevented from my original plan."

"And what about your brother?"

That question stopped me, but clearly López wanted to follow that subplot. "Well, my brother's situation . . . worked itself out," I said.

"Good, good." He seemed satisfied with that answer, unaware of how the topic had raised my own heart rate. But we sipped our beers and became a good deal more relaxed, and debated the rights and wrongs of some of the attitudes and assumptions we had been taught and had uncritically accepted, and how there was so much to learn from the traditions of those we might all too readily dismiss as "enemies." He wasn't quite ready to recommend the practice of always assuming the best rather than the worst intentions of those who cross your path. But he was surely getting there. I was amazed at how much we had both learned from one mule.

❧ 8 ❧

Fences and Defenses

I could see López was on a roll by now, so it came as no surprise when he arrived one evening unusually full of enthusiasm about the journey he had so recently embarked upon.

"You seem very fired up tonight," I said.

"Yes!" He smiled. "I finally let go of all that baggage that was holding me back. Let me tell you what just happened at Montserrat. . . ."

I wondered, strictly to myself, whether we can ever say we have shed all our baggage and whether his own future journey might disabuse him of some of this certainty, but that was for him to discover, not for me to preempt. And anyway, I was eager to learn what *had* happened at Montserrat.

The place in question is quite spectacular. A jagged ridge of mountainous molars bites into the Mediterranean skies and commands the attention of even the least observant of travelers. And López had made his way to that dramatic location—he could hardly have found a more appropriate backdrop for his grand gesture—with the purpose of making a full confession to the monks there and laying down all his worldly defenses on the altar of the famous Black Madonna.

"The confession alone took three days," he said. I hoped he would not run the entire script again in my living room. But when I recalled what he had shared with me about his misspent youth, perhaps three days was not, after all, excessive.

But soon we moved on to the real meat of the tale, as he described how he had laid down his sword and dagger—symbols of his former way of life—upon the altar. I couldn't help feeling moved by the commitment and determination shining out of his eyes. In fact, I wished I could have a bit of whatever he was on. I could easily visualize the weapons lying there on the altar, and the act of surrender they represented. It was a big deal, after all, to let go of everything you have depended on, everything that has shaped your sense of who you are.

"It was as if I were saying, 'This is who I have always thought I was. These are the accessories that defined my identity. Now I realize that I am both more, and less, than who I thought I was.'" The expression on his face was one of quiet acquiescence to something much greater than himself. I looked at my companion with a growing respect that went a great deal deeper than any admiration of his dramatic gestures. This man wasn't posturing; he was for real.

While listening to his story, I found myself wondering what defenses I might have been moved to surrender. My fingers moved toward my credit card, my car keys, my appointments diary. My protective affection assembled itself around my laptop and my passport and those other accoutrements that enable me to do what I want to do, travel to where I want to be, and live the life I want to lead. The images wouldn't go away. These things were my defenses against the unthinkable possibility of destitution, against the dreadful thought of becoming disconnected from the friends who give me a sense of self, against the gaping void of being someone whom no one wants to meet, to engage, to relate to. Not to mention the subtler, intangible threats to my self-importance and to the illusion that the world might not manage to turn without me.

I remembered how a friend, a former refugee, had once told me about his arrival in the immigration center with no ID, no birth certificate, no visible means of support. And how the official there had informed him that if he had no ID, he didn't exist. Do we really exist if we are stripped of all the outer layers of ourselves? Does our true identity disappear if it has no means of proving itself? Or does it, just possibly, become more, not less, real and true in its nakedness than it was in its dressing-up gear? Yes, I thought, our defenses go deep, and here we were, this stranger and I, trying to let them go.

My musings were abruptly interrupted when López, with a renewed burst of energy, told me about how, on his way to Montserrat, he had even given his gentleman's clothes away to a beggar in his determination to change roles and pursue his own life from now on as a beggar.

"Yes," I said, more to myself than to him, "when we have nothing left to be proud about, we can always be proud of our humility."

My blunt comment startled him a little, but then he nodded in agreement. "In fact, if I needed to learn that lesson, it wasn't long in coming. The poor beggar was arrested almost immediately, on suspicion of having *stolen* the clothes! Imagine that! When I meant so well, it all went wrong. I thought I was doing the right thing, expressing solidarity with a poor beggar by giving him my clothes, but actually I was putting up an even bigger fence between us. I suppose my gesture was saying, pretty clearly, 'Look at me. I have the good things you need, and I am so bighearted that I will give them to you. That will make me feel a lot better about myself. But how will it make *you* feel?'"

The question hung there in the air between us. Suddenly it wasn't just about a beggar and a cloak but about whole big questions of the haves and the have-nots and the gulf between them, about patronizing people when we really want to help them, about erecting fences when we really want to build roads, and about how little we truly understand about how to be the best we can be.

9

One Shoe On and One Shoe Off

I couldn't get out of my mind the conversation I'd had with López about defenses, about our need for security and outward signs of a person's identity and worth. My work was bringing up questions that I really didn't know how to deal with—matters of personal integrity and judgment. How far should I go in speaking my truth and encouraging others to speak theirs when this would inevitably lead to resistance and even opposition in some quarters? Indeed, the resistance and opposition were already coming up. I thought I might raise this painful topic with López at some point; our friendship had deepened, and his growth in wisdom made me more willing to confide in him about my journey. I imagined our next visit: him showing up at the door, his face bright with some spiritual discovery, his heart full of a new story to tell. He hadn't been around for days, and I found myself missing him, longing for his company. Longing for another mind and heart to help weigh my situation.

One morning, I heard shuffling outside. I drew back the curtains to see a street person standing on my doorstep. I opened the door, trying to decide how to respond to this soul's obvious need, and he simply walked straight in and settled himself down as if he owned the place. Not what I was used to from our local homeless folk, I must admit. The incident left me speechless, and I surveyed this derelict man, sitting in my comfortable chair, apparently feeling very much at home. He was dressed in rags that could have been some old sacking he had scavenged from the trash. His hair was frightful—dishevelled and dirty—and his fingernails were far too long and encrusted with grime. He had limped into my home, and now I could see that one foot was obviously giving him pain, and was shoeless, while on the other foot he wore a pilgrim's sandal. In that instant I recognized him.

"It's you!" I exclaimed.

"It's me," he agreed, with a wry smile.

I wanted to do all the right things—offer him the use of the shower, cut his nails for him, tend his damaged foot, but he gave me no time for any of this. Instead he launched into the latest twist of his extraordinary tale.

"I'm a pilgrim for God," he said. "From now on my life will be lived on the road, as a poor beggar, closest to those who are at the bottom of the heap. I left my old life behind on the altar at Montserrat. I am on my way to Jerusalem now, to help souls find the way to God."

He told me that, after making his definitive statement of intention and leaving Montserrat, he had made his way toward the little township of Manresa, intending to stay there for just a few days. And on the road he had met another "angel." Just as his beloved sister-in-law Magdalena had cared for him in his need, now another warmhearted woman had taken pity on him. The "honorable widow," Inés Pascual, had met him on the road from Montserrat and had clearly been moved by his strange mixture of beggar's garb and gentleman's bearing. She had directed him to a hostel where he could stay, and then—I loved this little detail—had kept him supplied with chicken soup to build him up and give him strength. Chicken soup for a wandering soul. Nice touch!

"So how is life in Manresa?" I asked. "It doesn't look as though you are exactly thriving there." I was unable to disguise my surprise at his matted hair and clawlike fingernails. He obviously picked up the direction of my gaze.

"I know I'm not exactly looking my best, and this is no way to turn up in your home. But the truth is, in the past I used to be very particular about grooming my hair—it had to be the latest style, and better than the latest style—and manicuring my nails. I feel sick to think about how much care I lavished on my appearance. So now I am trying to do the exact opposite and neglect myself in every possible way. My life was going down the wrong road entirely. I'm trying to get it on the right road in every way I can think of. The hair and fingernails are just a beginning. I'm sleeping on the floor to avoid any semblance of comfort, and eating as little as possible."

I looked at his gaunt frame, so different from the dashing young courtier I had initially come to know.

"So you are trying to hoist your life from the old road to the new," I said, to be sure I'd heard him correctly.

"That's about the truth of it."

"And it's impossibly difficult?"

"Nothing's impossible for God," he said with some vehemence.

"But for López, it just might be?" I wondered aloud. I decided to take the bull by the horns and risk his reaction. "Have you thought of a different possibility here?" I had the impression he had already definitively decided on the course he must take. "Have you considered that maybe God is in the process of changing the turns and intersections along your life's path, and if you let God just do that, then your life would quite naturally find itself on that entirely new road?

Maybe you don't have to personally heave the whole of your existence from one location to another, but simply allow the scenery to change in God's ways and God's time."

He seemed to be mulling this over. "Do you think I am trying to do it all myself?"

"What do *you* think?"

He smiled then. "You're a lot like my dear Inés, and other good women who have treated me with such mercy. Perhaps women by nature are better at waiting on God's grace. We men are so accustomed to getting things *done*—and doing it ourselves if at all possible!"

"I think God is pleased with your desire and even appreciates your effort," I said. "But what a gift to discover that it's not all up to us."

"Yes. I so easily forget God's grace, even though I have been so transformed by it already, even though it has worked miracles in my life already." He looked at me most kindly. "Thank you for reminding me. But I'm not sure how to proceed." He was gazing down at his feet.

"One of your feet is badly hurt and can't take the weight of your body," I said. "The other is sandaled and ready to walk alone. It seems to me that there is a part of you that is helpless and unable to move on your own strength, and the other side of you is absolutely determined to shape your new course on your own, the independent traveler who needs no help from anyone. One shoe on and one shoe off, just like your feet."

He smiled at the comparison. "There *is* a strong part—a good foot—I have to say. Some people are even coming to me for spiritual counsel, and I am doing God's work in the hospital, tending the poorest. And I'm putting in hours and hours of prayer, and constantly doing penance for the sins of my past life."

"Yes, that's the good foot," I said, "the one with the shoe. But I'm thinking that the helpless foot is the one God can really use. I think our failures and inadequacy are often closer to the heart of the matter than all our achievements. When we quit trying to do it all ourselves, because we realize that we *can't*, only then does the Spirit of God get a way in, and when *that* happens, stuff *really* happens."

He rose from the chair. "I understand what you're saying. But how will it work itself out?"

"Try putting your *worst* foot forward—offer to God the part of you that is weak and in pain."

He limped off into the night. Just before he disappeared from view, I called after him, "I believe God is changing your path even now, López!"

🙎 10 🙎

Crushed

I was cutting a few stray strands of lavender from the bush in the garden when López appeared. He looked subdued and even gaunter than the last time we had met, though, I must say, a bit tidier and more presentable. I think his friend Inés must have taken him in hand. He followed me inside and watched while I put the lavender in a vase and set it on the window-sill. Then he went over to it and inhaled deeply, relishing its fragrance.

"Isn't that amazing, the scent?" I said.

"You can't imagine what it means to me," he replied. "It feels like the breath of God, and I had almost come to think God was gone for good, or at least that I was forever banished from God's presence."

"It *is* a heavenly scent," I said, "but I once nearly blinded myself, when I was trying to tame that plant out there and got a sharp stick of it in my eye. What is sublime one minute can be lethal the next."

"*Tell* me about it!" He sighed wearily.

"Tell *me* about it if it would help," I invited him, as gently as I could, observing the wild and desperate look in his eyes—eyes that were red and strained, obviously from weeping.

What followed was a roller-coaster ride through the precipitous and dangerous terrain of López's past few weeks. The early months in Manresa, which had seemed so promising and given him glimpses of real joy and a sense of purpose, had been lived against a backdrop of his extreme penitential practices, so extreme that he had almost starved himself to death in his misguided efforts to purge his life of all that had gone before. Sublime moments of joy had given way to terrifying crashes into the depths of despair until the sunlight of spiritual consolation had disappeared, apparently forever, behind clouds of self-loathing and the darkest of thoughts.

"I'll never be able to keep this new life up for the rest of my days," he bewailed. "Imagine living like this for the next seventy years."

"None of us knows whether we will even live another day," I said. "Trying to second-guess the future is a pointless exercise."

"Hmm," he remarked. "That's what I said to the demons that were tormenting me."

"And did it help?"

"Eventually, yes, I think it helped. I just couldn't stop going over and over all the harm I'd caused in the past, and I convinced myself that there was no way God could ever use me as I had begged God to do."

"That's your ultimate goal—to be used? Is that God's ultimate goal, do you think? I thought God's greatest desire is to love us, not use us."

"Love?"

"I suspect that none of us is much use to God or to our fellow human beings until and unless we first let God *love* us."

"But how could God love a miserable wretch like me? I even hate *myself*. There's no way God can love me."

"Remember your dreams, when you were convalescing from your injuries and surgery, and how some seemed to come from a good source and others from a more destructive spirit?" I urged him. "Listen to those words you just said, these thoughts that are tormenting you. Which spirit do you think they are coming from, the creative, life-giving Spirit or from the destructive negative spirit?"

He looked up, but said nothing. It was obvious from his expression that he knew the answer. But could he follow through on it? Eventually his gaze came to rest on a mirror on the wall. In the few moments that passed, I watched his face crease into lines of extreme disgust with what he saw. It reminded me of a time many years ago when I could not even look into a mirror, so appalled I was at something I had done.

"It seems to me," I ventured, "that focusing on yourself does not really help at times such as this."

"But I need to focus—my *soul* needs to focus on all that I have to make amends for."

"But even repentance can turn into a form of self-focus. Isn't it better to focus on God and the love that forgives and transforms, than on those parts of our lives that are done with and can't be taken back?"

"Perhaps," he began. But it was almost as though a spiritual fever was gripping him, just as he had once been gripped by a near-fatal physical fever. I guessed the only way past it was to let it reach its crisis and trust that he would then turn a corner, change direction, recover his balance. But we were not there yet.

He fell to his knees and buried his head in his hands, leaning into the sofa. His heaving shoulders betrayed his attempt to suppress a fearful sobbing. My heart ached for him.

"I wanted to kill myself," he told me, through the shuddering anguish. "I was ready to jump. I so nearly made an end of it. I have looked into the abyss."

"And stepped back from it," I added, almost inaudibly. I moved a little closer. I rested my hand lightly on his shoulder, and then I noticed that in his fist he clenched a stem of lavender. He shifted and glanced at me as I looked at the stem. He looked at it too.

"It releases its fragrance when it's crushed," he murmured, more to himself than to me. "The crushing is the only prayer I can bring to you, my God, my God. . . ."

I knew that crushing. I remembered how the abyss had looked and how once another human being had held out a hand of loving care to me in my darkest hour.

"But you don't understand what I've done!" I heard my own voice echoing over nearly two decades. *"I had so much power over one life, and now have possibly changed it forever."*

"All the more reason to give this burden to God's greatness and stop striving with it on your own, in the awful privacy of your thoughts." I shuddered to imagine how my despair might have prevailed without the intervention of that wise soul, her strong words to me when I was in such conflict over choices I'd made.

Now I stood alongside López, wondering how similar we were in our painful pasts. We didn't speak—what was there to say? The minimal connection between my hand and his shoulder seemed to be just the slenderest of threads, linking us across our cultures, our histories, the five hundred years that separated us. Just a gossamer strand that compassion forged between us, but a strand as strong and invincible as any iron chain that Martin could have fashioned on his anvil in the smithy of López's childhood. Its strength and invincibility came from the Spirit of God flowing through it. Its fragility and its tenderness came from our own humanity. Together, these can draw the human spirit back from the brink of destruction to the threshold of new understanding. If I had ever doubted the wisdom of the mystics, that we are all interconnected, whatever time and space divide us, then from this hour I doubted no more.

❦ 11 ❦

Riverside Enlightenment

*M*y phone bleeped. I tried to suppress my irritation. I had other plans for this afternoon and didn't intend an unexpected text message to derail them. It was a lovely afternoon, far too nice to be inside. I was planning on taking some "me time" down by the river. So who was this, disturbing my peace, I wondered, as I groped for my phone and clicked "View" to reveal the culprit.

Can we meet at the bridge? Whenever you're free.
López

My first thought was how weird it is when a friend seems to read your mind and anticipate your desires. I texted back straightaway: "Sure. See you in ten mins."

Only when I was nearly to the river did the thought occur to me: How long would it take my service provider to get that message across five hundred years?

When I arrived, López was sitting on the river bank, hugging his knees. He looked expectantly in my direction and seemed unusually pleased to see me. I noticed that his hair was neatly trimmed, and so were his fingernails. He looked, actually, like a new creation. His eyes were shining, but with a gentle light, as if he were lit up from the inside. He invited me to join him, and for a few minutes we simply sat there in silence, gazing into the river.

"The river is *so* deep here," he said finally. "Deeper than the human eye can penetrate." His eyes were filled with tears, but they were the tears that flow from our deepest wells of joy, not the tears of desperation that had reddened his eyes so often recently.

"I love the river," I said. "I often sit here too and reflect on how it keeps on flowing, always the same river, yet you never see the same water twice. How it holds all our stories in its flow and yet is always revealing the present moment and calling us to live in it."

"It's a river that has given rise to the deepest experience of my life," he said quietly. "That's the river Cardoner near where I live and work, in Manresa. I can't describe what happened, but I long to share it with you. In fact, I long to share it with everyone I meet. Is this making any kind of sense?"

"It surely is," I encouraged him. "But some things just go far too deep for words."

He smiled, looking relieved to be able to talk about what lay so deep in his heart. And then he continued, as best he could, perhaps wishing he could turn it into a painting or a piece of music or a poem, yet stuck with the only medium we had—everyday speech, ordinary words to capture something of the supremely extraordinary.

"It wasn't a vision," he told me. "It was more like a kind of *knowledge*—but the knowledge that can reveal itself only through the heart, not the head. It was as though, in an instant—like a moment out of time—I understood everything in a new way. I could see new meaning in old truths, and a kind of simplicity and clarity in what had always felt like complicated matters, such as who God is, and what the Trinity means, and what the Eucharist is about. I couldn't even say in words what that understanding is. It just seems to have taken root in my heart, and from now on absolutely everything is different. I am different too. I feel much more truly who I really am. I can see things in a whole new way, and I really don't think anything is ever going to be the same again. It's like having a new mind and a new heart. But the tears just flow and flow, like my soul's river overflowing its banks and flooding my life."

I nodded because I understood, then took up the theme where he had left off. "It's as if some deep well has been pierced and a new energy is flowing up through that tiny perforation into the life we are actually living here and now," I suggested. "And that source of energy comes from way beyond ourselves, and yet is enough to fuel everything we will ever do or say or write from this moment onward."

His face registered surprise, and then real joy, that this conversation was possible between us.

"Whatever it is, it comes from the very source of God, and it makes everything come alive. I want to pray as I have never prayed before. I want to share this mystery with others so that they might be open to it themselves. I want to make it real in my own everyday life. I want to *live* it." He paused. "I wish I could remain in this heightened state forever, but you can't hold on to it, and you can't bring it back. Nothing you can do can make it happen."

"No," I agreed. "The Mystery does all the initiating. And perhaps that's a good thing." I was thinking of Jesus' friends who witnessed his transfiguration and wanted to put up shrines to contain the glory. "We can't catch it on camera or share it over the Internet; it lives its own life and does its own thing, and it feels like pure energy—an energy of total love and life and goodness and empowerment."

He nodded, gazing at the rushing water just below our dangling feet. "Do you think many people have moments like these?"

"More than we imagine, I'm guessing. But some wouldn't be able to name the experience or trust it and let it find a home in them."

"I want to call it *consolation without previous cause*," he said.

"In one of his poems, D. H. Lawrence calls it 'being dipped in God,'" I said. "But maybe we shouldn't try to call it anything. Perhaps we should just let *it* call *us*."

He sighed. "Yes. This grace is given for a reason. It comes with a call."

"It immerses us in God for a moment out of time so that God can immerse us in life, for as long as we live," I added. "I think that's how we know it is authentic. If such an experience truly comes from God, then it will make a difference, and not just for ourselves but for others."

We resumed our silence, both of us pondering what "immersion in life" was going to mean and what kind of difference it was going to make as our stories unfolded.

The shadows were lengthening now, and the intensity of light had already faded. We shook hands with a heartfelt *Au revoir.* López crossed the bridge that evening and disappeared into the dusk. He had crossed a threshold in every way. And the river blessed our meeting and our parting, our standing still, and our walking forward.

12

The Book

The spell of fine weather continued for a while into the changing season. On his next visit, López and I sat out on the deck, and for a while we simply soaked up the warmth of the sun and breathed in the scents of summer all around us. Above, a blue sky drew our hearts and minds beyond our own horizons, and down in the street all the noises of daily life hummed and hovered—shrill, gentle, complaining, conciliatory, shouts and whispers, groans, whimpers, and whoops of joy.

But change was imminent. The summer season would not last forever. Nature's mood would soon shift into a different gear, and so would López's onward journey. The glimpse of the unity of all things that he had experienced on the banks of the Cardoner would perhaps, in hindsight, be seen as a preparation for a hard path ahead, and the source of the energy that would be needed to walk that path.

My life was changing, too. Several of my engagements had fallen through, for political reasons, I thought. There had been a lull in the summer months I hadn't experienced since before I began giving writing workshops. I knew this was undermining my confidence and making me face uncomfortable questions, although every time I replayed my decisions, I could not think of any better alternatives.

There was also a more personal matter at hand. I'd been asked to take on a responsibility that I wasn't sure I could handle. There were strong reasons to do it and equally strong reasons not to. Not only the reasoning changed from hour to hour, but also my feelings about it. As a result I was feeling very unsettled.

But today was an interlude for simply being and enjoying the moment, and perhaps for taking stock, for sharing dreams.

López reached down and pulled a sheaf of papers out of his satchel. I had noticed that he carried this satchel with him every time he visited and wondered what he would bring out from it this time, but I kept my curiosity to myself.

"Remember our conversation about how you thought I was reading too many books and how maybe I should write one instead? And how you were kind enough to read some of my meditations on the Gospels?" he asked.

I recalled his earlier preoccupation with the romances of his day and remembered my throwaway remark, with a twinge of mortification, in the light of all that had transpired since. And I also recalled vividly how moved I had been to be offered a glimpse into his journeys into the Gospels.

"Well, my thoughts have moved on a bit, taken a new direction." He showed me the papers, rather shyly. "And I would love to hear what you think."

My eagerness was obvious. He smiled broadly, and then words tumbled out as he related to me the dreams that were shaping and guiding what he was writing.

He told me how, during the long months in Manresa, as he had been battling his demons and welcoming his angels, he had been making notes. He had been noticing the subtle connections between his exterior and interior life, and how certain thoughts and incidents might trigger precipitous plunges into his inner darkness while other things drew him toward the best in himself, and beyond. What had begun when he was convalescing from his injuries in the family castle, when he first noticed the profound difference between his superficial daydreams and the deeper "God-dreams," had now taken a much more definite form. He even thought the exercises he had been doing along these lines might be helpful to others. Hence "the book."

This kind of inner reflection on his everyday experience and his observation of the inner movements of his heart had become a habit and a systematic prayer for him. He had noticed that when the stirrings within him were in alignment with God's dream, he experienced a sense of resonance, or deep peace. When they

were not, then the experience was of an inner disso-
nance, and deep disturbance.

"You're saying that within a person there are signals," I said, trying to grasp his meaning. "That we
can know God's wisdom for us by attending to those
movements that happen inside us?"

"Yes. In fact, those movements are given as gifts.
What I mean to say is, God made us this way for a
reason."

"Made us what way?"

"Made us with the ability to have such spiritual
movements, and made us with the ability to observe
them and learn from them."

"Is that the same thing as a conscience?"

"It's that, but more than that. A person's conscience
is formed by her circumstances, her training, the exam-
ples set by parents and others who help shape her
when a child. And we know that not everyone is
shaped well."

"Certainly not." I was thinking of numerous people I'd known whose upbringing had leveled many
strikes against them. "And so, because conscience is

shaped by human experience, we can't necessarily depend on it."

"That's right. Everything I describe must be gone about with a prayerful spirit." I thought I detected tears in his eyes just then. "We ask God for the grace we need. We ask the Holy Spirit to guide us as we observe our inner movements of spirit. We must have God's help."

He grew silent at that. I was thinking of all my back-and-forth inner movements while considering the latest developments in my life. López's sigh broke through into my musing.

"As you know, there's much in my past to be guilty about."

"But God has forgiven you."

"Yes. God forgives and keeps forgiving. But because I was not trained all too well to use holy judgment, I have begun a practice I call the examination of conscience. I do it frequently—sometimes two or three times a day—asking for the grace to see whatever is not leading me closer to who I truly am in God."

I hoped that this "examination of conscience" wasn't going to precipitate the scruples and self-focused soul-searching that had plagued him earlier. He read my thoughts.

"You see, if I pause regularly and examine my life, I can deal with destructive patterns before they become persistent. I can weed out the behaviors and thoughts that move me away from God. I can realign myself as I go. I've found this extremely helpful."

I could see that his dream had taken a new and much more life-giving direction. It had been radically reshaped by his immersion in the life of Christ and in the Gospels themselves.

"I'm like a child in school," he said. "God is my teacher, and God is being infinitely patient with me, giving me these exercises to form my heart and mind into closer alignment with the divine dream."

I listened to all of this with a sense of growing wonder, but not, I admit, without an awareness of how easily the human heart can delude itself, how readily we can imagine that what we ourselves desire is also the Divine Desire.

Again I was struck by this man's uncanny ability to read my unspoken thoughts.

"Something I want to explore in the book is how we might ponder our own desires, at their very deepest, and learn to distinguish between superficial wants and wishes and the desires that express God's own desire for our lives. For example, I have noticed a difference in my own heart between what I call 'ordered' and 'disordered' desires."

"Ordered and disordered?" I said. "That sounds very . . . official."

"But listen. Disordered desires tend to be all about me and can make me greedy and possessive, taking what I think I want without any care for the effects on others or on creation as a whole. Ordered desires attract me toward what is life-giving, not just for me but for the greater good, and if I follow them, I not only do no harm but actually add to the greater good."

He paused, and I felt my heart pounding. I worked to keep my voice steady as I continued the thought he'd begun. "So I think you're saying that, in all we do, we either add to or diminish what is good in this world—what comes from love and hope and trust."

"Yes." He spoke softly, noticing, I suppose, the intense look I must have been wearing.

"And," I continued, "our very desires can help us discover what matters to us most, and whether that is fundamentally aligned to God and life itself, or merely serving our personal ends."

"Exactly," he said. "You could say we can choose to be at the center of our personal worlds or allow God to be there."

"I must say, López, this conversation strikes at my heart right now. My desires are so strong, and yet stronger forces seem to be pushing them back, preventing my dreams from living and thriving."

"Do you refer to your work—all the speaking and teaching you do?"

"Yes." I sighed then, and it was as deep a sigh as López had ever made in my presence. He looked at me intently, but his eyes were gentle.

"I try to help people write their truth," I said. "It is the burning desire of my life—because I believe we must begin with the truth."

"We must," he said. "Truth is reality itself, and we cannot invent another."

"Especially when a person writes his spiritual history, he or she needs to seek the truth and write it. Only then can any sense be made of it. And it's in the writing that often we see the real story for the first time."

"That's true!" he broke in. "So much of what I have learned of my own journey with God became clear as I thought upon it, but then even more so as I wrote it down."

"So you see my point. But not everyone looks at it that way. The trouble with truth is that it can be disturbing, and some people don't like to be disturbed."

"Is this why you are struggling in your work?"

"Yes, that's part of it—and I don't really want to go into it now. But through all that's happened recently, I've asked myself—and God—time and again if I was doing the right thing. I can't say that I've always heard

God's answer, but I've certainly come to the same conclusion every time."

"What conclusion is that, my friend?"

"That this work is important and it helps others, and I must continue."

"Your movement within seems quite clear."

"Yes."

"And you can see that it helps people on their journey with God."

"Yes, no doubt about that."

"Then there's your answer."

We gazed across the late summer day. I felt that something had been settled. "I can honestly say, López, that our deepest joy, the calling that's in the very core of us, is to live our lives centered upon the Source of all life, rejoicing in everything that gives life."

"Yet without clinging to life. We must learn to live lightly."

"Because actually everything is gift," I said. "We don't own anything. Even the things we think we own, we purchased with money that we earned by using—our gifts!" I surprised myself a bit with this revelation, but then I thought of children and of how a child possesses nothing except what she has first been given. Being grown up doesn't change that basic truth. "We have nothing that has not been given to us," I said, with sudden realization. It makes no sense to cling to things. It makes perfect sense to enjoy them and work with them while we have them, but to let them go graciously when we have to. In light of this, how successful my work was or wasn't didn't seem so important. "What kind of world might it be if our compulsion to possess things—and people, and power—could be transformed?"

"That's it!" he exclaimed. "That's my dream—to offer something to others that might make such transformation possible."

"All this very helpful—spiritual—conversation is making me feel thirsty," I said, getting up. "I could use a cup of coffee. You too?"

And I left him there with his manuscript, and went to put the kettle on.

✷ 13 ✷

A Way of Proceeding

*B*ut how does this work in practice," I asked, as we settled down to enjoy our coffee. "How do you actually *do* this work toward transformation?"

"I suppose you could call it a *way of proceeding*," he explained, as if that would clarify everything.

I looked blank. "Please tell me more. So far I am still not *proceeding* very well at all."

"I told you God is my teacher," he said. "And what God seems to be giving me is a kind of *process*, a way in which over time—maybe a lifetime—I might grow more and more like the person God is dreaming I can be. The book is my attempt to somehow capture that process so that I might be able to offer it to others, and they in turn might offer it to people they meet, who might be open to it. My time in Manresa has been like a long retreat, just me and God, and you could say these are my retreat notes. But I hope they are more than that. I hope they might serve as a guide to anyone who is offering these exercises to others. I want to try this for myself, give to others the exercises that have helped me, and these would be the notes I would use to help me to do that."

"But I still don't see how you would put these ideals into practice—actually begin to walk a path toward transformation," I insisted.

"You could see it as a kind of apprentice journey," he said, after stopping to think how he might plug the gaping holes in my understanding.

He began to unpack, then, what he called his *way of proceeding*. I listened with rapt attention as he began to outline the ways he had actually been learning to pray.

"The first and, I think, the most important step in the process is to get in touch with my ordinary experience and notice what is going on inside me, those inner stirrings I am noticing in myself. My passing moods and feelings can give me a lot of clues. If I'm feeling grumpy or irritated or angry, for example, I ask myself what lies at the roots of those feelings. Usually it's because the world isn't dancing to my tune. That can be a warning to me to look at where my heart really is centered in a particular situation and try to correct it if necessary, bring it back into alignment with what I know to be true. I look back over my experience every day like this and ask myself what has led me a little closer to God today and what has tended to draw me in the opposite direction. It's the most essential thing for me, even if I don't have time for any other kind of prayer."

That didn't seem so impossible, I thought. I should really try that. I might learn a lot about myself, and it sounded so *real*, so grounded in the ordinary world, that we could see and hear, touch, smell, and taste all around us, even as we sat drinking our coffee. Again, he intercepted my thoughts. "That's the heart of the matter: to discover the action and movement of God in everything and to respond accordingly. And to use all our senses to do so. God is in the aroma of this coffee as surely as in the laughter of the children over there on the playground. Everywhere! That's the gift: to see God in all things and all things in God."

"But there has to be more to it than that, surely?"

"Yes," he agreed. "We have to decide where our ultimate loyalty lies. Which king are we going to serve? Which flag are we going to rally to: the standard of God or the lure of evil?"

"We don't really do kings and flags and standards these days," I protested. "Especially women would have a problem with that, in an age that has been so destroyed by militarism."

"I understand that," he admitted. "But you would relate to the question of where you want your life to be centered—around what satisfies merely your immediate personal wishes or around what nourishes your well-being and that of the world generally."

"Yes, I can go with that," I said. "I would want my life to be centered upon whatever nurtures and loves all of creation."

"And having chosen which values you want to live by, the work then is to follow the one who embodies them, who shows you what it looks like in practice. In the life of Jesus of Nazareth we see what God's dream looks like in human form. In his suffering and death we realize what it costs to live true to that dream. And in his resurrection we envision the transformation that beckons us beyond anything we can imagine."

"Following isn't so easy," I said.

"I know," he agreed, with a heartfelt sigh. "But there are ways of praying with Scripture that really help us get inside the Gospels. As I said, it's like making an apprentice journey. Jesus is the Master, who teaches us by example how to live, and we emulate what we see in him. I have found that if I imagine myself right there in the midst of a Gospel event, I can become part of it, learn what it is teaching me about how to live my life, and even have a conversation with Jesus in my prayer, asking him for guidance. And you know what? When you do try to get inside the Gospels like that, actually the opposite happens. The Gospels get inside *you*, and *then* they can begin to transform you."

"And do we follow him all the way to the cross?" I asked, a bit nervously.

"At the foot of the cross is where we learn the most about ourselves and our response to God's call. There we learn how deeply we are complicit in those aspects of human activity that are death-dealing, and we also understand the depth of God's compassion for the ways we, ourselves, have been damaged. We meet our own helplessness, face-to-face, in the suffering of a helpless Jesus. We face our worst fears and most abject failures and see how God holds it all in loving hands, inviting us to step, with Jesus, across the threshold of transformation."

"Do you have a title for your book?" I asked him.

"It will be called the *Spiritual Exercises*," he announced with evident satisfaction. I refrained from suggesting that with a title like that it was hardly likely to make the bestsellers lists. Because, after all, time might prove me wrong.

"Tell you what," he added, with a gleam of delight in his eyes. "I end my book with a kind of exercise of thanksgiving, of surveying all that God has given us, and asking ourselves how we are going to respond, how we are going to love others, and all creation, with the kind of love that God reveals. Soon I am setting out on a long journey, and I know you are going to be traveling to distant shores too. Why don't we celebrate? Let's have dinner together tomorrow. A thanksgiving dinner, for all we have shared so far, and a promise feast for the journeys ahead of us."

Any excuse for a party, I thought. And this was a better excuse than most. In fact it sounded like a most satisfactory way of proceeding.

❧ 14 ❧

Thanksgiving Dinner

*I*t was a great evening. He brought the food, and I brought the guests.

Food seemed to appear effortlessly, as he glided in and out of my apartment. A pot of Inés's famous chicken soup—I couldn't wait to try that! Fresh-baked bread, still warm from the oven! How did he do that? Salad from someone's garden, so fresh that the dew-drops were still gleaming on the lettuce leaves. Spanish tomatoes, straight from the vine, olives, and apricots. A bowl of freshly made guacamole. French cheese—a concession to Pamplona, perhaps. And a large carafe of Spanish Rioja.

We greeted one another with a welcoming hug and sat down to our feast. I began by lighting a candle. "Let this candle be a symbol for us of the Source of all life and light and love. Everything at our table, everything we have and call our own, everything we are, flows from this Source. May the candle remind us of the holiness of all that is, and all we share."

We rested for a few moments in the silence and the light, each acknowledging its meaning in our own way.

"This is a thanksgiving feast," said López, breaking the silence eventually. "So why don't we begin by remembering what we are thankful for."

We sat a while longer in quiet reflection, not searching for something to be grateful for but wondering where to begin. Gratitude was truly overflowing tonight.

"I am grateful for the journey my life has made so far," he began. "I am grateful for the way God intervened and changed, point by point, the course of my life's path, to bring me to a completely different place from where I was just a couple of years ago. I'm especially grateful for the things I got wrong and for my weaknesses, because they were the entry points for healing and for grace. I am grateful for the fact that I can put my past behind me and start afresh, forgiven. I am grateful for everyone who has given me the means to live while I have been begging for food in Manresa. I am grateful for the mule who taught me how much wisdom I lacked." He said this with a sideways smile in my direction. "And I am grateful for this chance to journey with you, Rachel, through our conversations together."

"It's mutual," I said. "I enjoy our meetings so much, though when you first arrived I didn't know what I was getting into. I am grateful for the reality that time and distance mean nothing when we engage with each other authentically from the heart. When I look at this feast spread on my little table, I want to thank the universe itself, the sun and the rain, the earth and the changing seasons, the cow for the milk that made the cheese, the gardener who grew the salad, the avocado that surrendered its independence and consented to merge with the lime to make this guacamole, the grapes that offered themselves to be crushed to give us this fine wine, the hen who gave up her life to become this soup and for Inés, who prepared it for us. When I taste this feast, I hear the universe itself saying, 'This is my body, given for you.' I think tonight we are sharing in the simplest and most profound communion of all—the communion of all that is, giving and sharing itself with all."

López's eyes were bright with tears. His expression opened, as it so often did, to hear and learn any new turns of phrase, any fresh vocabulary for God's love and our communion in it.

I continued. "But when I take this and eat it, the body of life, broken daily and freely given for me, this asks for a response from me. This meal gives me energy—energy that has been given at great cost by other creatures. So how will I respond? How will I use the energy this sacred meal gives me? How will I spend it, for the greater good?"

López raised his eyebrows and looked at me as though I had hit on the key question. How will we spend the love we are given? And this, I felt, was the right moment to introduce our guests. Our table was set for two, but there was a third place, empty, except for my laptop, which lay open on the placemat. I leaned over to switch it on and to bring up some clips from YouTube. I think López thought that my mind had wandered off topic for a moment, but soon he was riveted to the screen.

"Meet Joy and Steve, my neighbors," I announced, clicking the Play button. We watched together as Joy introduced the latest batch of children they were fostering. "Nobody prepares you for the awfulness of some of their stories," she said. "This little girl was born addicted to heroin and was taken from a mother who didn't want to know about her. This little fellow was born in a high-security jail. His mom isn't coming out anytime soon. They are troubled, and they keep us on our toes all the time, but we reckon if we can make a difference to just a few young lives, it is worth everything. And really, the only thing they long for is love."

The next clip brought Colum to our table. He was standing by his window, overlooking a busy industrial port where he was the chaplain. Every day mariners from all over the world passed through the port, and his love for them was written all over his face. Often they had not been paid for months, and sometimes they had not been given decent rations. He made it his task to obtain justice for them while they were onshore. "I want everyone who sails from this port to leave here having experienced that life means well with them and that there are people who care," he said.

The scene changed again. We were in the inner city, at a homeless shelter. Eileen was caring for the sick there. "I beg too," she said. "I try to persuade medics to volunteer one morning a month to come here and help tend the sick who have no health insurance. There is no shortage of volunteers. And this is my good friend Mary. She has started a school for young girls from the ghettos around here, where they can have a chance to escape from the poverty and violence and deprivation and get a high school education, for a new start in life." "I am a beggar, too," Mary admitted. "I call it fund-raising, and people are amazingly generous. The school is flourishing." Mary is not well herself, but she rarely thinks about her own limitations. The vision that fires her heart keeps her supplied with all the energy she needs to keep on caring for "her girls."

Our final guest is Eithna, a cook in a retreat center in Ireland. Eithna is in love with the universe and every creature in it. "Did you know that there are trillions of bacteria in one teaspoon of soil?" she asked, with a gleam of joy in her eye. "And they are all working nonstop to make the soil fruitful so that it can give us potatoes and carrots and beans. I absolutely love my work. When I stand at my workplace and chop these good vegetables, and prepare this meat and stir this soup, I am taking what has come from the dust of the earth and transforming it into luscious lunches. I feel as though I am working with God to add life and joy and vitality to the world, and I hope that all who share in the table here will relish every morsel and know that they are participating in the holy as they enjoy their meals. I hope that at the end of every day the world will be a little bit more nourished and delighted through what I so enjoy doing."

As Eithna faded back into the Wicklow hills, López and I both began to eat more slowly and reflectively and with much greater relish. As we took and ate this food that the earth had given and human hands prepared, we knew in a new way that we were participating in a sacred act.

López was obviously moved by these encounters. He seemed not to notice the tears trickling freely down his face. Only when I noticed his tears did I realize that I was tearful, too. These were surely the tears that accompany consolation!

"Our guests show us how deeply true it is," he said, "that love shows itself in deeds and not just in words. They are loving those in their care with God's own love. May we live true to this challenge in our own lives as we journey on. May we be carriers and multipliers of love."

And, simultaneously, we said, "Amen."

"Let's light two smaller candles from this bigger one," I suggested. "And let each of us carry one of them away with us as we journey onward from this moment. Let it be a symbol of the love we long to bring into the world, and let it remind us that we carry God in our hearts and God carries *us*."

I watched as López walked slowly off into the night, a circle of candlelight dancing around him as he went. And I wondered when, and where, we would meet again.

🙾 15 🙾

Moving On

*I*f you want to disappear for a while into anonymity, an international airport is just the place to do it. The crowds will swallow you whole, and the probability of bumping into someone you know is satisfyingly low. Unless, that is, your circle of acquaintances embraces other space-times.

I passed him as I paced the miles from security to boarding gate. It was the cloak and the sombrero that caught my attention. Not your average traveller, I thought. Not towing some smart little cabin bag, just a satchel over his shoulder. Where had I seen that satchel before? For a few moments we walked parallel paths. Both alone. Both on foot. But his shoes were made for walking. Mine only needed to get me to the gate of my departing flight. I was on my way to a group of people who, in inviting me, had provoked the criticism and opposition of some of the religious authorities there. We had had to change locations for the retreat to a place not under the jurisdiction of those authorities. So as I walked steadily toward my flight, I vacillated between worrying about the retreat and trying to assess the situation of the man keeping pace with me to my left. He looked like a traveling scholar who had landed in the wrong century by a freak oversight of air traffic control. He was making his way across Europe. I was travelling to the other side of the world, backpack on my shoulders. I felt a conversation coming on.

"You're looking a bit thin," I commented, while nevertheless beaming my pleasure at seeing him again so unexpectedly. He had been gravely ill, he admitted. But now nothing was going to stand between him and Jerusalem. Though, he added, he wasn't telling people that the Holy Land was his intended destination. It might appear presumptuous to be undertaking such an arduous journey. We passed the EL AL desk, and

I smiled to myself. What a difference half a millennium makes.

Things had become difficult in Manresa, I learned. There was talk—well, actually typical small-town gossip. People were murmuring, and not in a friendly way, about this stranger, especially about his odd habits and his friendships with women. Inés had conferred with her brother, a bishop, and they had advised López to move to Barcelona, under their protection, while planning his onward journey. His eyes softened as he recalled the Manresa months, despite the cloud hanging over their conclusion.

"Manresa has been my training ground—what you might call a novitiate," he said. "God has been teaching me, and Manresa was my kindergarten."

"If all you have shared with me so far was the kindergarten," I ventured, "then I wouldn't want to know how the high school will be."

"Who knows?" he murmured. "But these months have helped me visualize a plan, a shape, in what I must do, and what I might recommend to others."

I could see that we were looking at a "way of pro-ceeding" again, and I listened closely as he described a six-point plan, right there in the sterile corridors of twenty-first-century aviation.

Point 1: The *Exercises* were quite definitely the starting point and the whole heart of the matter. The encounter with God that they facilitated in the person who made them was the key to everything else. The fruits of this encounter would then take shape in very specific ways (he was nothing if not specific!).

Point 2: Serving the sick in hospitals. López's life in God was absolutely grounded in his life among the poorest of his fellow human beings.

Point 3: Making a pilgrimage on foot. I flinched a little at this one, thinking of my forthcoming "pilgrim-age" of twenty thousand miles.

Point 4: Working at humble tasks. I mentally translated this into "seeing how the other half lives," if only for a limited time, and thought about how most people, especially women, do this all their lives.

Point 5: Teaching others about the ways of God. No small undertaking, I thought, and wondered whether offering a few retreats here and there might count.

Point 6: Caring for souls.

"How would you do that?" I asked with genuine interest.

"Most frequently by means of conversations," he said, "in which I mainly listen very carefully and attentively, and only then respond to what has been shared. It's in conversations like these that people often reveal the things that most concern them—often the things that are keeping them distant from God."

"What you describe—this type of listening and companionship—we call it spiritual direction now," I said.

His eyebrows rose. "That's an interesting phrase. Although we must be very careful *not* to direct but to help the person hear *God's* direction."

"Those who train to be spiritual companions are taught exactly that—to get out of the way, as you have put it so well."

He smiled, looking satisfied, but then fell silent for a while. I could sense his sadness when he said, "It's really hard to leave things behind, to let things go. It's like a little dying every time."

"Do you mean the moving around you do, from one place to another?"

"Yes. I care so deeply for those I leave behind—although I know that wherever I go, I will find others, and genuine caring will develop into friendship."

I thought back to the people I keep having to leave behind, and the places I wish I could stay in, and the clock I would sometimes wish to halt in its inexorable onward march.

"I guess this is God's lesson too," he added philosophically. "Learning to let go, and to move on."

"But moving on, well, that isn't so easy, is it?" I asked. "It isn't at all obvious where the path is leading or which way to head."

"Jesus left home and set out into the unknown, letting the Father guide each day," he remarked. "Jesus was learning on the road, as he went, and so will we."

He said it with a conviction that I wished I felt, especially about that little word *we*.

"Apprentices, then," I said. "With a Master to teach us, and a way of proceeding that he reveals to us through our own personal experience."

He said nothing, but the serenity of his smile said it all. Then he continued his story. In Barcelona he was living in a small room, on almost nothing. He ate sparingly, prayed abundantly, and begged for what he needed. In fact, he had been severely admonished by one worthy lady, who advised him that it was shameful to beg if you were capable of earning your living. Secretly I was inclined to agree with her, though in López's case perhaps an exception might be made, given his assiduous labors in teaching the young and tending the infirm.

"Who's paying your airfare?" He suddenly fired the question at me at point-blank range, reading my unspoken thoughts. "The people who invited me," I sputtered, a bit taken aback. He said nothing more, but left me to ponder the various conjugations of the verb *to beg*.

He was waiting for a ship to take him to Italy, and he had met an influential lady, Isabel Roser, and her nobleman husband, who had persuaded him not to take the first ship that was due to sail, which they considered unseaworthy. López was still struggling to come to terms with the fact that this first vessel had precipitously sunk, still in sight of land, with a total loss of life. Isabel Roser would become a dear friend and benefactor and a mixed blessing, but that would be another story.

For now, this man was entrusting himself entirely to God. This gave me pause for thought. Many things go through my head during the tedious hours of a long-haul flight, but never once has it occurred to me to doubt the competence of the pilot. Why, then, do I so regularly fail to trust the Mystery that holds trillions of galaxies in balance?

My flight was boarding. I turned to say bon voyage, but he had disappeared into the anonymous throng, trusting God, and leaving me to trust the pilot.

❧ 16 ❧

Obstacles

*D*isgruntlement sat upon López's brow tonight as though it were a permanent resident. At our last encounter he had been fired up for his pilgrimage to the Holy Land. Tonight he certainly didn't look like a pilgrim suffused with the light of one who has touched his heart's desire. We sat for a while in silence as I waited for the story to unfold in its own time.

The joy and the spiritual consolations of actually setting foot upon Terra Sancta when he landed at Jaffa found expression more eloquently in the tears that flowed across his cheeks than in his words as he sat there in his favorite chair, hands folded in his lap, eyes lowered, savoring the memories of those momentous days.

But getting there at all had been an obstacle course, and staying there had proved an impossibility. He had set sail from Barcelona for Italy in springtime, just about a year after his first arrival at Montserrat. Was it really only a year? So much had happened to him, and in him, during that short year. And so he had embarked on his first long sea trip. Once in Italy, he had made his way to Rome to get papal permission to go to the Holy Land.

"How wonderful!" I said. "Italy is so very beautiful in spring!"

"I really wouldn't know," he said. "The Plague was raging through the country. No travelers were allowed within the walled towns. Itinerants were definitely not welcome!" But after an arduous journey, sleeping rough and begging, he had eventually arrived at Rome at Easter.

"One night I well remember," he said. "I was sleeping in a stable. I had been walking together with a woman and her daughter and a young man. We were all begging our way, and that night we had met with some soldiers who seemed very kind, inviting us to share their fire and food. The soldier in me came on duty when I saw that. I was suspicious of the way they were getting familiar with the women. I know how soldiers can be, so I slept with one eye open, just in case. And sure enough, in the middle of the night I heard screams and rushed out to find the women outside in the courtyard, terrified, and claiming that the solders had tried to rape them. I was furious. I was as wild as when I was defending Pamplona, and the soldiers ran off into the night. So, what with the Plague and the hazards of life on the road, and all the red tape that had to be negotiated to get a chance of a passage from Venice to Jaffa—well, yes, I began to lose heart. I still had to get a passport to enter Venice, and for that I had to go to Padua, and even then there was a good chance I would be refused."

"So did you make it to Venice?"

"One night I had another experience of the closeness of God and the presence of Jesus," he said, as if that would answer my question. "I felt completely reassured that all would be well if I carried on trusting in God. And you know what? At Padua they never even asked for a health certificate. I got the passport without any difficulty. Why had I ever doubted?"

I stopped in my tracks. "You call that doubt?" I said, thinking back over the reckless trust he had placed in God every step of the way. He stopped too, and looked into my eyes, and for the first time I really registered the sparkle in them. His eyes had a light of their own.

"When I got to Venice, I slept under the porticoes in the Piazza di San Marco," he went on.

Prime location, I thought to myself. Nothing but the best for López!

But then—Jaffa! And the fixed intention of never returning to Europe. From now on he would live his life in the land of Jesus, plant his feet in Jesus' footprints, bring God's love to this sacred land, give his *Exercises* in "God's own country," gather companions who together would bring this lost land back to the heart of God. He had it all worked out.

The air of certainty with which he described these intentions was already ringing warning bells in my mind. Life rarely runs according to our arrangements.

And sure enough: in Jerusalem the irresistible force met the immovable object. López and his unstoppable determination came up against the rigid rule of the Turks, who had the Holy Land firmly under their control, and a wandering Christian pilgrim such as López figured absolutely nowhere in the scheme of things. He had hit an impassable roadblock to his high intentions.

And if he had hoped for an ally in the Christian Franciscan presence in Jerusalem, his hopes were quickly dashed. All his arguments in favor of his settling permanently met the full resistance of the Franciscan provincial, who summarily ordered him to leave, for his own safety and under threat of excommunication.

But he wasn't going to go quietly.

"I had visited Gethsemane," he told me, "and I needed to go back just once more."

I could so understand this kind of last-chance feeling and desire, until he added, "You see, Jesus' footprint is there, the print he left behind when he ascended to the Father, and I had to check out the exact direction that footprint is facing. I even gave the guard a pair of scissors as a bribe to let me in."

I kept quiet as my frustrated, literal-minded little friend held my gaze. Why was it, that given so many differences in our way of seeing things, we were becoming more and more deeply bonded in genuine affection? I felt for him in the shattering of his dream, in spite of his pedantic pursuit of a footprint. He was gradually teaching me, and perhaps himself, that following in the footsteps of Jesus was a bigger deal altogether than either he or I had imagined.

And so a "lifetime in the Holy Land" had amounted to just twenty days before he was ignominiously sent back to Spain. "Man proposes. God disposes," I said as we parted. Remarkably, he was still able to smile at this ironic twist in his tale. "Then so be it," he said, and left.

✤ 17 ✤

Back to School

I was running late. Having forgotten that it was the first day of school and the roads would be congested at this time of the afternoon, I was stuttering through the traffic, squeezed between the suburban 4x4s transporting their little Jimmies and Janes back home, when I caught sight of something very strange indeed. A throng of small boys, perhaps about twelve years old, were jostling an older man, who was stubbornly walking in the midst of them. The satchel he carried marked him out as an oddball who had slipped uncomfortably into the wrong time, place, and age-group. He looked as though he was trying, without conspicuous success, to be one of the boys, but they, in their turn, were mercilessly pushing him around and mocking him, and even tugging at his clothing. I felt sorry for the poor guy, even though he surely didn't have to be there among all these juveniles.

I pulled over and pulled him into the car. That satchel was the giveaway again. He seemed relieved, and after I had given the kids a piece of my mind, we drove off, leaving them laughing at our backs. But he seemed quite phlegmatic about the whole incident, as I offered him coffee and waited for any explanation that might, in due course, be forthcoming.

"I wasn't an easy student," he suddenly announced as I passed him the cream. "God had to take me in hand in my kindergarten time in Manresa, and Master Ardevol had his problems with me too, in Barcelona." I wondered where all this was leading, but I knew better than to ask.

"My life seemed to be going round in circles." He went on to admit that after the failure to get a toe-hold in the Holy Land, he had lost any real focus, and this had concerned him—until realization had dawned, with a clarity that so often characterized his discernments. What he really needed was to get the education he had spurned in his younger years.

A worthy objective, my twenty-first-century mind agreed, imagining him enrolling for some Adult Ed. program. But no! He had gone back to first principles, found Master Ardevol, a teacher in Barcelona who was willing to take him on for free, and attached himself to this class of young boys in order to learn the rudiments of Latin grammar and literature. He was a man of thirty-three in a class of boisterous adolescents, whose idea of entertainment was to torment this little man sitting on the floor in their midst.

"An exercise in humility as well as grammar?" I said.

"And also in concentration," he added.

This bit of the preposterous story surprised me even more. He didn't strike me as a man with learning difficulties. He noticed my raised eyebrows and went on to explain how his attention was constantly distracted by spiritual thoughts. His immediate inclination was, naturally enough, to welcome them and let them draw him into prayer, and consequently Latin was tending to fall by the wayside.

"Contemplation and action need to go hand in hand," he told me very firmly, as if I, not he, were the transgressor. "However much we feel drawn to prayer, we must still put our very best efforts into our everyday responsibilities. It's prayer that fuels our actions, but our actions are the fruit that prayer brings forth. I realized that I was letting contemplation take over and neglecting the action." And "action," at this juncture, had meant chanting Latin verbs with twelve-year-olds! A far cry from Pamplona.

And so he had promised his teacher that he would never miss a class or fail to be attentive as long as he was able to find bread and water in Barcelona to support himself. And for two years he had honored this promise.

But in his struggle to balance the consolations of prayer with the conjugations of Latin, he had learned something else. He had learned to recognize "the devil in disguise." Sometimes temptation comes to us in the guise of something that is in itself good—even very good. The consolations of his prayer were clearly very good indeed, but he had recognized that at this time of his life he needed to focus all his energy on acquiring the education that would enable him to serve God and "help souls" more effectively in the future.

"Temptation is a tricky business," I commented.

"Indeed it is," he said in an unusually somber tone. "The forces of darkness that would deceive us can dress themselves up very cleverly to look like something good and true."

I recalled an email I had received only that morning, purporting to be from the Revenue service, telling me that they owed me a refund—a very unlikely but welcome surprise—and asking me for my full banking details in order to make the repayment. Fortunately I, too, had recognized "the devil in disguise" and had stopped short of delivering this data into the hands of a fraudulent hacker.

Eventually, López had reached a standard at which he was considered ready to enroll for the Arts course at Alcala University. This had opened up a whole new

range of learning opportunities into which he had joy-
fully immersed himself.

"But now, as I said, I am going round in circles,
rushing from one lecture to another, wishing I could
be in two places at once, trying to take in everything,
and no one to guide me," he said wistfully. And yet this
situation would also be a place of learning in a way he
had not bargained for. I listened eagerly.

"Non multa sed multum," he muttered. If I had
not known him better, I might have suspected him
of showing off his newfound Latin competence, but
his face was serious. "Quintillian said that," he added,
almost apologetically. "It means it is better to study one
thing in depth than to dabble superficially in many
things." This was probably the most important thing
he had learned at Alcala, he thought: the need to focus
and the importance of an ordered approach to study.
It was wisdom I knew I badly needed myself in my
distracted lifestyle. Regrettably these insights had come
too late for his time at Alcala to be fruitful. But there
were other obstacles awaiting him of an even more

serious nature. And other challenges of student life that would open up a whole new horizon of possibility.

He left in a rather downbeat mood, but still trusting in the God who had brought him this far. It was dark as he set off back into his own century. No children on the streets to plague him now. Just his own thoughts.

18

Tensions

*L*ópez comes across to me as the kind of person who explains things by marshaling whatever objects come to hand. Thus, salt and pepper shakers, sugar bowls and creamers, napkin rings and cutlery are all good allies when he wants to make a point. I guess it's the soldier in him, or the commanding officer.

This was the mood tonight. Not argumentative, but enquiring, exploring, and striving to reconcile apparent opposites.

"Tensions!" he said emphatically. "So many tensions and so hard to reconcile them."

I waited quietly for further specifics to emerge. It was then that he began to rearrange that bit of the world that lay within easy reach, on my table.

"My first experience of serious tensions has shocked me," he revealed, his face turning white in the process. In fact, his face is often a color-coded guide to his feelings, sometimes red with excitement or anger, sometimes white with apprehension.

"Here am I," he went on, "convinced beyond question of the reality of God's touch upon my life and of God's personal guidance in the call to help souls and to bring straying hearts and minds into true faith in the bosom of mother church. But suddenly I find myself accused by that same church—under suspicion and investigation and even imprisoned and silenced!"

"Accused of what?" I felt color draining from my own face.

The catalog of allegations sounded shaky to me and uncomfortably familiar to a twenty-first-century ear. He had been suspected of being influenced by the "Alumbrados," or "enlightened ones," a group of people who suggested that God deals directly with individuals and not just through the offices of the institutional church. He was suspected of intending to open up a "parallel path" to God by forming a new religious group. He was accused of "being different"—not wearing the right clothes, not going about his ministry in the usual way, standing out in the crowd. And underneath it all lay the obvious, but unspoken, charge: he was a nonordained person speaking of the things of God in nonconsecrated places and attracting large crowds eager to hear the divine invitation in a fresh, simple, and life-changing way. The powers that be feel threatened in such circumstances. They close ranks. They accuse, investigate, and silence the one who is different. In López's case, they had put him on trial three times in Alcala, held him prisoner for forty-two days, made him dye his clothes, dress normally, and wear shoes, and had forbidden him to continue teaching until he had completed four more years of study.

"Conformers always hound the nonconformers," I said, my blood now rising.

He smiled ruefully. "In Salamanca the Dominicans turned on me and put me under house arrest. I was more than happy for them to investigate my *Exercises*. I wanted nothing more than to be found free of all heresies."

"And were you?"

"Eventually, yes," he replied, "But they forbade me to teach on the differences between mortal and venial sin until I had studied for four more years."

"Well, at the heart of your *Exercises* is God's love and forgiveness," I said. "Let others work mightily on their definitions of sin."

He noticed, then, that I was really taking this conversation to heart. I could feel the heat in my face, which meant that my cheeks were turning crimson.

"What is it?" he asked.

"It's just that what you are sharing is connecting so much with my own experience. I've mentioned how my work has been running into problems recently. Well, those problems can be related quite directly to certain accusations leveled against me."

"And what accusations would they be?"

"Not so different from those you have faced, although there's no official religious institution questioning me, just a few individuals with the power to cause a stir."

"Do they charge you with heresy?"

"Not quite. But they don't like it that I encourage people to connect their sense of the divine with their experience of everyday life. They don't like that I am welcoming and inclusive toward any sort of person who wants to be involved. Basically they don't like laypeople like me doing the kind of work I do, because they have no control over laypeople. Worst of all, though, is how these accusations threaten to discourage the people I'm trying to help."

"Do these accusers speak directly to the people who attend your retreats?"

"No. People like that don't work directly or transparently. The criticism is more subtle and insidious. They just put obstacles in the way, like refusing to allow workshops to take place on their properties. Not once has anyone come out openly and discussed things with me personally. They simply close doors against me or try to discourage people from attending."

"What are you doing at these workshops that is so . . . controversial?" His eyes were wide with surprise.

"I simply create a safe place in which people can write their truth. As I've mentioned before, sometimes the truth is disturbing, and sometimes honesty raises questions, and sometimes people who ask questions are threatening to those people who like to make rules and tell the rest of us exactly how God's will must be played out."

López shook his head, sighing as he did so. "But you know yourself how often the great saints of God were demonized before they were canonized."

"Well, López, that's hardly my concern. The last thing on *my* mind is sainthood!" I shuddered at the very idea.

"I know that," he reassured me. "But anyone who longs to help souls is a saint in the making—and often a provocation to the religious authorities." He saw my expression and added quickly, "Oh, I don't mean the canonized kind. You and I, and many, many others listen to our soul's deepest desires, and we go where those desires lead. And sometimes they lead straight to trouble, don't they?"

And then he started to mobilize his little army on the table. "Just look at how these tensions stack up . . . between obedience to authority and freedom of conscience, between respecting tradition and also moving forward."

The pepper veered to the right of the table while the salt lurched to the left. I made no comment. I wasn't going to step into the fray.

"And then," he went on, "the tension between trusting God absolutely and for everything, and the need to use our own initiative. I know I need to study and acquire intellectual knowledge, but that can be at odds with the deeper imperative to reflect on my actual experience and allow myself to be guided by knowledge of the heart—that personal conviction and passion that fire me from within."

At this, the knife aligned with the pepper, and the fork joined the salt.

"And as my—as *our*—life has moved on,"—he was on a roll by now—"I feel the tension between maintaining personal friendship with my companions and at the same time encouraging them to be available to work in God's vineyard anywhere in the world, where I may never see them again. And I feel personally caught between wanting to remain just an ordinary person finding God in the ordinary things of everyday life, and realizing that if I am to be left in peace by the Inquisition, I am going to have to toe the institutional line, even to the point of studying for ordination. A mere layman really has no voice!"

And the sugar flew east with a vengeance while the creamer marched vigorously west.

"Tensions, tension, tensions . . . between the center of the church that holds it all together and those who walk the edges, where fresh growth happens. Between living a life of prayer in the cloisters and walking with God on the streets. Between rejoicing in created things and being willing, if necessary, to let them go. Between experiencing opposition and not becoming embittered. Between knowing when to resist and when to surrender. Between surrendering to human control and surrendering only to God."

His voice was rising to a crescendo, and the napkin rings scurried furiously to one or the other of the opposing flanks building up on my embattled table.

"Will we *ever* resolve all these tensions?" He aimed this question first at heaven but then glanced pointedly at me, I suppose because we were now partners in a tension-beleaguered world. All I could do was raise my eyebrows, agreeing to question right along with him.

Then he suddenly spotted my guitar standing in the corner of the room.

"You play?" he asked.

"A bit," I admitted.

"I love music," he said. "Would you play something for me?"

I agreed, with some embarrassment, less than confident in my own ability.

López fell silent and listened intently, growing calmer by the minute.

"That's it!" he said when my little musical interlude petered out. "You've put your finger on it. My desire is

to unite the human instrument with God, to bring my human self into resonance with the divine harmony and help others do the same. Your guitar knows more about this than we do. The music itself is the result of tensions. If the strings are not taut enough, there will be no music. If they are too taut, they will snap. My God!" he proclaimed with a yelp of joy. "Tension can be *creative* if we learn to hold it in balance. No tension equals no music. It's not about *eliminating* tensions but about *balancing* them. All we need to do is *hold* the tensions and let God make the music."

With a flourish, he swept the opposing armies together into a temporary truce, cast a broad, contented smile across my ravaged table, and took off into the night.

19

The Beggar Student

Why Paris?" I asked him as he settled down with his coffee, a superannuated student full of the joys of the French capital.

"Why Paris?" he repeated, incredulously. "Why? Because Paris is the cultural and intellectual crossroads of Europe. To study in Paris is to be exposed to all the crosscurrents of thought that are reshaping human society and culture everywhere. And anyway," he added shrewdly, "it's a bit further away from the grasp of the Inquisition. What's more, I can't speak French, and I knew that this limitation would curb my pastoral activities and force me to get down to some serious study (in Latin, of course) without any holy distractions." He grinned.

I returned his grin. Only López could think that not speaking French would be an advantage in Paris.

I was wondering how he had financed this new venture, but he supplied the answer before I could ask the question.

"I even had some funds," he told me. "Isabel Roser had sent me twenty-five gold crowns. It looked as if I could hold my head above water, but not for long. There was this friend, Mazores, another Spanish student, and I asked him to look after the money for me. I thought I could trust him. But when I needed it back, he had spent it and couldn't repay it."

"That couldn't have done much for your friendship with him," I commented.

"Oh, it wasn't such a big problem." He brushed it off as if it had been a minor irritation. "C'est la vie! I was used to the beggar's life, so I went back to it. I didn't hold it against him, once I got over the initial shock."

"So where did you live, without money?"

"In a poorhouse," he said, as if such an outcome were self-evident. "That wouldn't have been a problem except that I couldn't go out in the morning before dawn or return after dusk, and that meant missing an early and a late class. So I ramped up the begging circuit. I went further afield. Even got as far as England."

"Really?" I raised my eyebrows.

"Yes! And they were very generous to me there. Thanks to benevolent donors, I was able to leave the poorhouse and move into the College of Sainte-Barbe. Not that that was much of an improvement, but at least I could get to all my classes."

"And how have you enjoyed la vie parisienne?" I asked.

"It's been a curious mixture of studying hard and helping souls." Obviously the lack of French had not been the insuperable obstacle to his extramural activities he had hoped! "I've been able to give my *Exercises* to several people, with very good effect. In some cases, *too* good. Three students, after making the *Exercises*—"

"Excuse me, did you say *making* the *Exercises*?"

"Yes, that's how I describe it. These intense and prolonged practices of prayer I call *Exercises*, as you know. So we've come to say that when a person is going through them, he is making the *Exercises*. As I was saying, three students who completed making the *Exercises* decided to sell everything and take a vow of poverty. Fine, of course, but it brought the wrath of the Inquisition down on me again. I was accused of unduly influencing them, which really wasn't true. That's not how the *Exercises* work—at the heart of these spiritual exercises is the nurturing of one's individual prayer with God. In fact, I try my best, when leading people, to stay out of their way! So when these students opted to sell their belongings, it was entirely their decision. But I was blamed, being older and therefore assumed to be wiser than they were. That very nearly cost me a public whipping." His voice dropped at the very thought.

My heart sank at his dilemma. Bizarre though his methods might appear, this man, I knew, was utterly sincere and totally committed to attending to God in the people he met. I would have trusted him with my life, though I had known him for only a few months. I was appalled at the idea of his being publicly whipped, and the horror showed in my face.

He seemed to appreciate my unspoken concern. "I wasn't afraid of the whipping," he assured me. "I'm used to pain, and to humiliation. What concerned me was that others would be deterred from making a radical choice for God if they witnessed this spectacle. I told the rector so. I challenged him to think about the effects of what he was about to do."

"And then?" I was eager to hear the outcome of this unlikely confrontation between an undergraduate and his rector.

"He saw my point." López gave a little smile. "We came out of that conversation like a pair of old friends. The show was off."

He fell silent for a while as he savored his coffee. Finally, he spoke. "I've taken the rock."

I cast a glance out to my little garden, but all its features seemed to be still in place. "You've taken the rock?"

"That's how they do the final degree examinations," he explained. "I think it's supposed to be about humility. The candidate has to sit on a stone at the feet of the examiner for the duration of the examination. Once an interview is over, he then carries his rock to the next examiner and repeats the process. I question how much these people really understand about humility," he wondered aloud. "Humility forced by one who has power over another is not humility but humiliation. Humility in the presence of the power and the love of God is something entirely different—an attitude of mind and heart never forced but freely given. But whether you like it or not, 'taking the rock' is the way you take a degree in the University of Paris. My problem wasn't the requirement to sit on a stone, but the financial cost. For poor students, the cost of graduating is prohibitive. Without the help of benefactors I couldn't have done it, and really wondered whether I *should* do it. It felt a bit like colluding with a corrupt system. But I need the intellectual credentials if I am to pursue the ministry I feel God is calling me to."

I didn't say anything but thought immediately of some of the humiliations that can be imposed on people by those who have authority over them, both in the corporate and the ecclesiastical worlds. Actually, what López had just described also sounded strikingly familiar—minus the rock—to what many a student endures while pursuing a course of study, especially in expensive and prestigious universities!

López shuffled a little uneasily in his chair. Much of what he had shared resonated with my own experience as well. The issue of restricting access to tertiary education, through exorbitant fees, could have come straight out of the present time. And the disturbing moral question of how far we are colluding with false systems when we go along with their demands was an issue very close to my heart. Many of the sponsors and hosts of my work were related directly or indirectly to one of the largest and most powerful organizations in the world.

But our conversation ended on a much happier note.

"The greatest gift of my time in Paris has been the gift of friends," he told me. "Next time I come, I'll introduce you to some of them. I think you will love them."

20

"Ours"

I still haven't quite grown out of my tendency to worry about what other people are thinking! That tendency was dramatically reactivated when I spotted López walking up the path, followed by no less than *six* of his friends, all attired in much the same style as he was. The strange thing is that despite all the medieval comings and goings at my little apartment, nobody has ever said anything or appeared even to notice anything. So maybe I would get away with it again today. I opened the door and stood amazed as they all piled in.

I recalled a friend of mine who always kept three chairs in readiness on his deck. "One for solitude, two for companionship, and three for company," he always said. Two had been company with López through all our conversations. Eight of us, in my tiny apartment, was definitely a crowd. I wasn't sure how I felt about this sudden change of chemistry. Something told me that from now on my relationship with López would have to expand to embrace this circle of friends.

López invited them to make themselves at home, and that somehow warmed my heart. He obviously felt at home here himself, and that said something about our growing friendship.

"Meet my two roommates!" he said, introducing two young men in their early twenties. One, a blond, studious-looking, but very charming young man, he introduced as Pierre Favre from Savoie. His family were peasants, and he had started his life as a shepherd boy but had longed to study. Now, very shy but possessing a deep presence of peace, Pierre seemed full of admiration, and gratitude, for López, who had clearly had a powerful influence on him and helped him find direction for his soul and his life.

As Pierre modestly withdrew into the background, López reached out to draw forward his second roommate, Francis Xavier. Francis and Pierre had been roommates for four years before López had turned up at the College of Sainte-Barbe. Francis was sharp and athletic, a social charmer, full of energy. His childhood had been clouded by family tragedies he had witnessed and the destruction of his family home, a castle in Navarre, where his people would have fought on the opposing side to López in the battle at Pamplona. But this didn't seem to have marred their friendship.

"I thought he was a joke at first," Francis told me, smiling broadly at López. "I used to chafe him about being a middle-aged God-botherer. Couldn't get him involved in athletics or interested in the Paris nightlife."

"Francis was a hard nut to crack," admitted López. "Very aloof at first, and scornful of my dreams. But I understood him. I could relate to his desire to win every contest that was going. I'd been there myself. I knew that one day he would discover that there were other trophies to strive for, other goals to attain; not for ourselves but for the glory of God. And I'm glad to say, he's getting there."

A small young man of twenty-one came next, closely followed by a slightly younger boy. "This is Diego Lainez," López announced, of the older of the two. "And here is his friend and mine, Alfonso Salmeron. They are from Alcala in Spain, and they don't speak French, so we are kindred souls in foreign lands." Lainez held out his hand in greeting. "I'd heard of López back in Alcala," he told me, "so imagine my joy when I bumped into him quite by chance in Paris." *No such thing as coincidence,* I thought, as I studied Lainez's features. He seemed buried in the depths of his own learning, but his eyes were wide and full of expression as he held my gaze. Here, I thought, was a genuinely holy man, small in stature but an intellectual giant. He had, I learned, already obtained his master's degree from Alcala University.

Alfonso Salmeron was very different, full of fun, open and outgoing, a native of Toledo. "Get him to recite his Greek and Latin poets for you!" López was clearly proud of his friend's accomplishments. In spite of, or maybe because of, their differences, Lainez and Salmeron were inseparable friends, complementing each other's personalities and united in their shared enthusiasm for the values that López was teaching them and the vision he held out to them.

Next came a hotheaded, impulsive-looking youth called Nicolas de Bobadilla. "I'm from Old Castile," he informed me abruptly. "I came to Paris to study with the best academics and to become fluent in the languages I need. López has been a big help to me in making the right contacts." Bobadilla was nothing if not direct about his intentions and aspirations. "He needs a bit of restraining," López interjected. "I had to warn him to watch out that his chosen teachers were sound in their orthodoxy. Left to himself, he'd get into all kinds of trouble."

"Well, the Dominicans and Franciscans should be sound enough, even for your rigorous standards," Bobadilla retorted.

"And last but not least, here's our scholarship boy," said López, introducing me to a young Portuguese man, Simon Rodrigues, whose eyes betrayed a volatile personality. "It's true," said Rodrigues, smiling. "I've been here in Paris for seven years on a scholarship from

King John III of Portugal, and I moved in with López four years ago. But it's only recently that I've been drawn to seek out his spiritual counsel. I knew I could share something of my deepest dreams with him and give him part of my soul. He's just the kind of person who inspires that kind of trust. I know now that this friendship is taking my whole life in a new direction."

I looked around my lounge, which seemed to have taken on the character of a student hostel, alive with youthful energy and buzzing with discussion and friendly banter. There was something unspoken that bonded these friends together. On the face of it they made unlikely companions. Their backgrounds differed wildly, and so did their temperaments. Perhaps they noticed the questions that were forming in my mind. What was it that they held, each separately in their hearts, but that somehow formed an invisible web of deep relationship between them?

"We are discovering that we all have a dream," said Favre at last. "Most of us have made López's *Exercises*, and in every case our lives have been transformed. We meet together now, each of us committed to following

Jesus, but also committed to one another and to the dream of 'helping souls,' however that might work out in practice. We are good companions, for sure. But we are more than that. We are companions of Jesus."

"Thanks for welcoming *ours*," López said as they were leaving. And from then on, whenever he talked about these special friends, and others who would later join the circle, he called them simply "ours."

𝒮 21 𝒮

Picnic in Montmarte

On the next visit, I found López gazing at a charcoal sketch of me when I was seventeen. It hangs in my hallway, but this was the first time he had noticed it.

"You look so alive, your life ahead of you and a dream shining in your eyes," he remarked.

"I was just coming to the end of my school days," I told him. "I went with some friends to Paris to celebrate, and an artist did that sketch up in Montmartre, in the artists' quarter."

"You know Montmartre?" he asked, with awakened interest.

"Well, just to visit. But I love it there. It's a very special place."

"For me, too," he said, thoughtfully.

I guess I looked puzzled, because he went on to explain how he and his circle of friends had also held a celebratory gathering in Montmartre back in 1534.

"We had reached a landmark moment in our own studies in Paris," he said. "There was still a long way to go, but we knew we had arrived at a significant moment in our friendship and in the dream we all shared for a future that would be very different from our past lives. Like yourself, we were full of energy and enthusiasm for the life that lay ahead, and there was a dream shining in our eyes too. Looking at that portrait reminds me of how often we climbed the steep hill of Montmartre, how we roamed those narrow lanes and alleys and gazed down at the vista of Paris spread out at our feet. It reminds me of the eagerness and the commitment of our youthful hearts. Well," he added ruefully, "at least the others, the six friends you met, were youthful. I was very much the old man of the circle, but I was no less fired up than they were."

"What were you dreaming in those youthful hearts?" I asked.

He smiled. "We had already decided, each of us individually, to dedicate our lives to the service of God in attending to the needs of God's people; to care for the sick, instruct the young, and to live in total poverty. We also discovered that we each cherished the dream of going to the Holy Land to help souls in the land where Jesus had lived. We used to meet in one another's rooms and share these dreams. It was very strange," he mused almost to himself, "how each of us had reached the same decision independently."

I glanced up at the sketch. At that time I had been standing on the verge of a great adventure. I had been full of ideals and aspirations. Now, I suppose, many years later, some of those dreams really have taken concrete shape, but many have been stifled and suppressed. I really hoped the dreams of López and "Ours" would grow and bear fruit and not be stifled by the weight of time and circumstance.

"It was the fifteenth of August, 1534—the Feast of the Assumption of Our Lady," he continued his story. This Catholic feast day would have been a pressing reason for the friends to attend Mass, even if there had not been a still more pressing, more personal reason. On this day, he told me, they had resolved to turn their collective dreaming into a solid vow. They had taken themselves to the church of St. Denis in Montmartre in order to pledge themselves to God and to each other, and to sanctify their plans for a future to be lived together in the service of their fellow human beings.

Pierre Favre was the only one who was ordained, and so he celebrated the Mass that day, and before they received communion, each of them in turn offered his solemn vow to this end. When the time was right, they would try to go to the Holy Land. Should this not be possible, they would offer themselves instead to the pope, to be sent wherever he deemed the need to be greatest.

"We were on top of the world that morning," López said, eyes sparkling. "Up there on the heights of Montmartre, we were also on the threshold of a whole new way of life. We celebrated in grand style, with a picnic in the park."

I wondered what the artists would have made of that photo opportunity if they had been there then.

"You have more confidence in the institutional church than most people have today," I said. López looked at me quizzically. "You think so?"

"Well, it sounds to me sometimes as though you would maintain that even if something is white but the church says it's black, then it's black. No argument."

He hesitated. I wondered whether five hundred years in heaven might have modified his certainty on this point.

"The church is another name for the people of God," he said. "I think that now I would express my conviction that in the depths of the human heart there is a rootedness in the divine that knows what is right and wrong and knows when it is in alignment with that deep center and when it is straying. This is the ultimate existence in God that I urge people to trust, and to trust it more than they trust any immediate and sometimes unreflected answers to life's mysteries."

"And religious institutions in their visible, organized forms, are clearly just as likely to stray from that deep truth as any individual," I suggested.

"The forms that we put around these deep mysteries can easily become *de*formed—you remember our discussion about things being disordered?—and therefore constantly need to be *re*formed," he said. "They are temporary and man-made, and they can gravely limit our understanding. But the Mystery itself is pure and changeless and utterly to be trusted."

"Just as St. Francis realized," I interjected, "when he was setting off to join the papal armies in the holy wars of his time, thinking that this must be the 'right' thing to do, and heard a voice from heaven warning him to 'follow the Master, and not the men.'"

López nodded. "Wise words," was all he said.

22

Home Leave

*T*here was something different about the view from my window today. At first I couldn't work out what it was. Then I spotted it. Someone had tied a rather attractive little chestnut horse to the park railings opposite my apartment. We don't get many animals visiting in this particular part of the suburban jungle, so it caught my eye, and I wondered who it might belong to. I didn't have to wonder for long. The rider came up with a bucket of water for his horse and patted it lovingly before turning away and heading for my front door.

He had lost a lot of weight, but he was still basically his old, rather compact self, a high color in his

.

cheeks, his reddish-blond hair balding, and sporting a long beard. He was wearing a rough brown robe and rope-soled sandals.

"I see you've upgraded to business class," I teased, pointing to the horse.

"That was my friends' idea. I really didn't want it. I intended to go on foot as I usually do," he insisted, with a glance at his calloused feet that had already walked the length and breadth of Europe. "But my health hasn't been great, and they wouldn't hear of it. They decided I needed a break back home in Loyola, and to get me there they presented me with this splendid beast."

"Sounds good," I said. "No harm in some rest and recuperation in the place you love best. How did it feel to be back home?"

"I wanted to keep the whole thing very low profile," he said. "I wanted to go back to the place where my earlier life had caused so much scandal and bring a good example instead. And," he added in an undertone, "there were some affairs I needed to settle."

Was it my imagination, or did he turn a few shades paler as he mentioned the word "affairs"?

"I would have arrived unnoticed," he went on, after this uncomfortable moment, "if I hadn't been recognized by someone from home as I journeyed. He must have told my family I was on my way, because my brothers sent out an armed escort to conduct me safely home. As if I need an armed escort!" His glance shot upward, indignant. "I've got God."

Okay, I thought, *confidence is everything.*

Listening between the lines, so to speak, I picked up the impression that López's time in Azpeitia, his hometown, had caused quite a stir. For starters he had insisted on staying in the local beggars' hostel instead of lodging in the castle at Loyola with his family. I could imagine that going down like a lead balloon. Then he had set about ministering to the folk of the town and seemed to have won over their hearts and minds. He gathered the children around him and instructed them outside the Magdalen hospital. He touched the sick and suffering with a healing hand and worked to reconcile many who were estranged, including a bit of counseling to married couples.

Like Jesus before him, he had certainly comforted the afflicted, but he had also afflicted the comfortable. He told me, for example, that he had challenged some of the young ladies of the town who were openly claiming to be the wives of priests and were wearing the appropriate head covering to prove it. He assured me that many had reformed their wicked ways.

"Did you also challenge the 'husbands' of these 'wives'?" I asked. But that thought didn't seem to have occurred to him.

"The people flocked to hear the word of God," he said, deftly changing the subject. "People really do have a deep hunger for the things of the spirit, in my day, as in yours. Sometimes I would even preach to them from the top of a cherry tree."

I could hardly suppress my laughter at the thought of this little man up a cherry tree proclaiming the ways of the Lord—the non-ordained preacher in the non-consecrated pulpit. And yet, I thought, here was a man clearly called by God to do what he was doing, and in following his call, he was revealing to ordinary people the sacred nature of their ordinary lives. What clearer ordination, what greater consecration could there be than this?

"The people were generous," he went on. "They plied me with all kinds of gifts, but I was determined to accept only what I absolutely needed. One day a gift of fresh fish and oranges arrived from a woman I had helped. At first I told her she should sell the goods and give the money to the poor instead. But she was having none of it. She absolutely insisted on my taking it, and in the end I had no other option."

"It's sometimes harder to receive than to give," I said. "God may love a cheerful giver, but for there to be a cheerful giver, there has to be one who gladly and gratefully receives, don't you think?"

"This is true," he said. "I accepted her gift, and that night we had a grand fish and orange supper party down at the hostel." And he dissolved into laughter at the memory.

I must admit that seeing him so happy brought mixed emotions. Could I ever go home again? I wondered. How welcome would I be? I had left home under a cloud of family disagreement—mainly about my younger brother, Ricky, who even then was running wild and causing so much heartache. My parents and I had disagreed vehemently over how to handle things. In their eyes he could do no wrong, and they cast me as the cruel older sister. What's more, they disapproved of my marriage. When I left there were no tears shed by any of us, and the estrangement had continued, unhealed.

"It must have been quite hard to leave Azpeitia," I said, dragging my mind back to López and his story, "not knowing whether you would ever go there again."

"They did ask me to stay on. But I think they and I both knew that my mission had to go beyond this one valley, however much I loved the place and its people. I hope they will remember me, as time goes on. Before I left, I arranged that the bells of the parish church and the surrounding shrines should be rung every day at noon for the Angelus, to call the people to a moment's prayer in the midst of their working day. It's a good habit to get into," he added, "especially in your frantic world today. Just a few minutes reflection each day, to reconnect to the sacredness of ordinary life. It doesn't even need a bell."

Night was falling when he left. I went to the window to watch him ride away, but the horse had gone. He walked off into the night as usual on his calloused feet. Puzzled, I went to clear away the cups and found a note under the coffee pot:

"Don't worry about the horse. I left it behind in Azpeitia as a farewell gift. Would you believe that it was still there sixteen years later? Two friends who had been passing through told me they had seen it there, enjoying a happy retirement."

23

Of Tears and Stars

Tonight, there was a power failure, not an unknown or even an infrequent event in these parts. Probably the sudden onset of cold weather had caused a surge in demand, and so we've been left to freeze until the supply is reconnected. Not the situation you hope for when visitors call, but López's visits are so unpredictable that the weather forecast really doesn't enter the equation. I welcomed him into my dark and chilly apartment, but it didn't take us long to realize that we would be much more comfortable walking outside than shivering indoors.

It was a dry, crisp evening, and the streets were quiet. Everyone else must have been sitting out the power outage wrapped up in blankets in their own homes. We preferred to walk ourselves warm. López was a walker, for sure. At first I could hardly keep up with him, but as the night worked its magic on us, we both slowed to a more reflective pace. The stillness soaked right into us, and we fell silent. Overhead the stars were suddenly so bright, in the absence of any artificial light, so close that you felt you could have plucked them down like silver apples from a celestial orchard. We gazed in silence for what seemed like a breath-taking eternity.

There was a faraway smile on López's face as he surrendered himself to his own rapture, before eventually breaking the silence with words spoken almost inaudibly.

"How often have I gazed at the stars," he murmured. "I can't describe what the sight of the stars does to me. They invariably bring me close to tears. Shining specks of light in the heavens—how amazing they are, beyond human counting, beyond human probing or understanding. They seem to be countless in number, and who can guess at the mystery that holds them in balance?"

"Now we know that there are billions of them in our galaxy alone," I said, "and that there are about two billion galaxies in our universe. The numbers are utterly mind-blowing. And now, with today's telescopes we can even see how stars are born and how they die in great supernova explosions, scattering stardust into space, and this same stardust holds the very elements of which our own bodies are made. In our physical nature we are literally made of stardust."

López was speechless. Such revelations stretched his mind beyond all sixteenth-century reason, and yet he clearly possessed a mind that was eminently capable of, and open to, being stretched. We stood there side by side, filled with wonder, each in our own way and our own time zone. When he turned to me again, the tears in his eyes reflected back the starlight. It reminded me of a night in the Australian outback, when the stars were visible in their billions, and the Milky Way stretched like an eternal river right across the sky, pouring from north to south, holding the brilliance of the Southern Cross like a celestial monstrance proclaiming, "All this is my Body!" And by day we had rejoiced to see the bush carpeted in wildflowers, the "everlastings," or paper daisies, beloved of the West Australians, and it had seemed to me that for every flower there was a star and for every star a flower, and all was one, in daylight and in darkness, in life and in death.

So, too, did López's tears mirror the stars he loved, and the stars became a part of who he was, and shone from his eyes in the sparkle that I had come to know and cherish.

"We are able now to send out signals into deep space," I told him, "in our attempts to communicate with any intelligent life there may be elsewhere in the universe."

He looked at me with an incredulous expression, and I felt unaccountably embarrassed by our twenty-first-century determination to probe the secrets of creation. Something seemed not quite right here. I felt like a fly walking across the surface of a great work of art and imagining it could ever understand its mystery and meaning.

"You are trying to make contact with all this?" he asked, holding up his hands, prayerlike, to the sparkling heavens. "But what if it's the other way around? What if all this mystery is actually trying to communicate with *us*?"

I was silenced for the second time this evening. Whatever I thought I could see with my present-day eyes and modern mind, this little man, with his classical education and absolutely no scientific knowledge, could see much, much more through his tear-ravaged eyes and in his medieval mind.

It was my turn to be incredulous. "How could that be?" I asked him. "What could make you think this mystery is trying to communicate with us?"

"Don't you feel that if it is a matter of searching for intelligent life, the mystery that holds all of this is infinitely greater than anything we could possess in our human minds, or even imagine in our wildest dreams? Isn't it more likely that such infinite intelligence is much more able to communicate with us than we with it?"

"You sound as if you really *know* what it might mean for this mystery to communicate with you," I said.

"I only need to listen to the stirrings within my own heart, and I know it is so," he said with absolute conviction. "I don't need your technology to do that. I just need stillness of spirit and an open, receptive heart. Then it isn't hard to recognize that the infinity of life pulsing through the galaxies is the same pulse of life that keeps me living and breathing."

"Perhaps this is what the Mystery is trying to tell us," I said, turning my gaze skyward again.

"Let those who have ears to hear listen to its call," he added, "and those with eyes to see behold its glory. May we remember that we live and move in sacred space."

24

Fears and Favors

My heart sank when I opened my door tonight. I thought for a dreadful moment that López had regressed to some of his earlier habits of self-neglect and even self-harm.

"Whatever happened to you?" I asked with alarm, as I took in his mud-spattered clothing and dishevelled appearance. But his eyes belied the general state of him. They shone with a glow that seemed to come from deep within. With scant regard for the effects upon my furniture, he flopped into his favorite chair.

"You know what?" he began. "When I was young, I was afraid of absolutely nothing. Or at least so I believed. The hazards of war held no power over me.

No enemy could intimidate me. I stood my ground. I have walked all over Europe and never paused to consider the dangers I might have been walking into."

I can hear a "but" coming, I thought.

"But on my way to Bologna, I was compelled to face my fears."

My concerned expression must have encouraged him to go on, because he then told me about a peculiar series of incidents that came in quick succession and on which he had reflected deeply. The first happened during a sea crossing from Valencia to Genoa.

"People tried to put me off," he told me. "Barbarossa was threatening the coast, and I knew it wasn't safe to sail. But I wasn't going to let a mere Turkish pirate push me off course. In the end, it was a quite different hazard that made me tremble. The ship's rudder broke in a fierce storm. We all thought we were facing certain death at sea."

My heart froze at the thought. I imagined how I might feel if the steering in my car were to fail on the highway, leaving me with no control over the consequences.

"How did it feel, to be looking death in the face?" I asked.

"Well," he said, thoughtfully, "I have to say that when the storm was at its height, I looked back over my life and felt acute sorrow. Not for my many sins, so much, but for not having made much better use of the many gifts I have been given."

What a change, I thought, from the man who in the past had been so focused on his shortcomings, to this positive and mature person whose main concern was to make full use of his gifts. Oh, that we all could go through that kind of change.

"But you clearly survived," I remarked. "Those mud splashes didn't come from a shipwreck."

"Right!" he agreed. "And I am embarrassed to tell you how I acquired them."

The story then unfolded of his travels from Genoa to Bologna in the depths of winter, when the roads were quagmires and he had found himself on a narrow cliff path in the Apennines.

"It was the kind of path you travel in nightmares," he said. "The higher I climbed, the narrower the path became, and below me the river was raging and rising in full flood. I had to crawl along on my hands and knees, literally clutching at straws for fear of falling to my death. I felt paralyzed by fear, unable either to go back or continue onward. I swear that was the most terrifying moment of my life."

"I wonder what that fear was telling you about where your life was going," I found myself saying, for no apparent reason.

He looked at me quizzically, as though waiting for further elucidation.

"Well, it's just that your story so far seems to be carrying you forward into a new stage that is unpredictable, without an obvious rudder, and potentially bringing you into situations where you will find yourself, as we would say today, between a rock and a hard place."

"Hmm," came the noncommittal response. "You may be right. If so, I hope the next incident wasn't a sign of things to come. As I was just entering Bologna—can you believe it?—I was crossing a little wooden bridge across a small creek, perfectly safe and harmless, when for no reason at all I fell off, splash, into the water. Imagine, after all the terror on the cliff path, to fall into a creek and get soaked to the skin and covered in sludge."

"A mortifying entrance," I agreed in sympathy.

"And it didn't get much better. Everyone had a good laugh at my expense. After that I got nowhere with the begging in Bologna. Not a penny. Not a crust. And after I had provided them with such a good day's entertainment! And then the grim, cold fog set in. I fell sick again—the old stomach trouble. So after a while I decided to move on to Venice, even though there was still more than year to go before the time the companions and I had agreed to meet there and plan our future together."

"Even so, there is something quite amazing in your eyes tonight," I said. "It hasn't been all mud and mortification, has it? I wonder where that inner glow is coming from."

"I think I can tell you more about that," he said, after further thought. "It was some good while later, after a quiet year in Venice, catching up with correspondence and thinking through my plans to offer my *Exercises*. Something remarkable happened to me on my way to Rome. A profound favor from God! God touched me again in such a powerful way that my own fears, about the future and the unknown dangers that might be waiting around the next corner, seemed to dissolve into insignificance in comparison. Something so remarkable that I will save it for our next meeting. Right now I am going to get myself cleaned up."

With that, he was gone.

❧ 25 ❧

La Storta

*L*ópez was gone a very long time. So long that I began to fear I might never see him again. My own travels had taken me to the other side of the world. López was the last thing on my mind as I sat on the terrace of a little retreat house in South Australia. Here, the first Jesuits to come to Australia had arrived from Austria and established a vineyard. The director of the center had explained to us how it got its name. Full of Roman zeal, these men had come here with the full intention of "bringing Rome to the south." They had found this place, with its rolling meadows and hillsides where vines might thrive, and seen in it the seven hills of Rome. So they had called it "Sevenhill." The little river that flows nearby they had named the Tiber. And the house itself, being just outside their "new Rome," they named "La Storta" for a place close to the old Rome. Presumably well satisfied with their achievement of imposing a bit more of Europe on this vast and ancient land, they then got on with the job of "helping souls" and growing grapes.

Today the sting of imperialism has long departed from this place of prayer and reflection, and the grip of Rome has mellowed into a loving spirit, welcoming to all who are searching for deeper meaning in their lives. The house is in silence, and people wander through the meadows, making their own journeys with God, and each evening the Eucharist is celebrated by one of the resident Jesuit priests.

Tonight it's different. None of us has ever seen the presiding priest before. Well, no one except myself, and even I have to do a double take. Could it possibly be him? I hardly recognize him in his priestly outfit. But yes! His face lights up in greeting, reflecting my own surprised delight.

Afterward there is a tap at my door, and there he is, bearing a bottle of Sevenhill wine and two glasses. It promises to be a convivial evening.

"You never cease to amaze me," I tell him. "I didn't know you were ordained. How did that happen?"

"I can tell you *where* it happened," he said. "It was in Venice, on June 24, 1537, feast day of St. John the Baptist. And I and several of 'ours' were ordained together—you remember meeting Lainez, Bobadilla, and my dear Xavier—we were all there, also Cordure and Rodrigues. All six of us were ordained. That was where it happened. As to how it happened, well, that is a bit more complicated."

I was eager to hear his explanation. What had made this extraordinary layperson, so clearly filled with a divine spirit of compassion and wisdom, suddenly want to become ordained into an ecclesiastical organization that was hugely compromised by corruption and decadence?

"I realized already in Jerusalem that if I was going to be free to help souls in the way I felt God was asking me to do, I would be able to do so only under the umbrella of the official church. As a layperson I was going to be blocked all along the line. And anyway," he added, noticing my dubious expression, "it needed reforming. We all felt that to reform it, we needed to live an authentic priestly life inside the system, like leaven in the dough, you might say, to bring a new and more Christlike vision to the church of Rome."

"So you might say you were the protestants and reformers *inside* the Roman system, not unlike those trying to achieve the same result *outside* it?"

"Well," he said, smiling, "I've never been called a protestant before, but since you put it like that, yes, it was a way of protesting against a system that was so rife with abuses. But I always loved the church, and to be able to celebrate the Eucharist meant a great deal to me. It meant a great deal to be able to celebrate here tonight, in La Storta, of all places."

"Why La Storta?"

"I promised, last time we met, to tell you about what happened just outside Rome—the original Rome." He smiled as he filled up my glass. I sat back, eager to hear the story.

"It was already October, in 1537. There were three of us," he began. "Lainez, Favre, and myself. We had all felt we should go to Rome, but none of us was totally at ease with this. Lainez had become very ill, so much so that I hired a horse for him. As for myself, I was not in a good place at that time. We all still cherished the dream of going to Jerusalem, to serve God's people there. So the matter of Rome was troubling me, and I felt confused and plagued by doubts. I wanted to do God's will, not follow my own, but there was this uncomfortable feeling that somehow the plan to go to the Holy Land would be subverted."

"I walked on ahead of the other two, alone, and at a fast pace. I think my speed shocked them a bit. But I needed to be alone and try to discern the right way forward. Eventually I came across a tiny chapel on the roadside not far from Rome and went inside to pray and beg for guidance. I was feeling pretty desperate, I can tell you. What did I most deeply desire? Was it to go to Jerusalem? Or was it to do God's will, whatever and wherever that might be? My longing for guidance crystallized into a simple prayer: 'Please place me with your Son,' I prayed. That was all. That was it. The little place where I found the chapel was called La Storta! So being here now, in this second 'La Storta,' has a very powerful significance for me.

"What happened next felt like an earthquake inside me," he continued. "There could no longer be any doubt. I suddenly knew—really knew, as if I had physically seen and heard it—that the Father had indeed placed me with the Son, asking him to take me with him on mission, wherever that mission might lead. I fell to my knees in awe and gratitude, but with a lot of apprehension as well. What was this going to mean? And then came the next moment of clarity. It felt as if Jesus himself said to me, 'I will be favorable to you in Rome.'"

"What do you think he meant by that?" I asked, after a long silence.

"Who can tell?" he said. "It could mean anything. It could even mean crucifixion, like it did for Peter!"

"My God!" I said. "And you trust that?"

"I trust it absolutely," he said, draining his glass. "I know it's from God. And I trust it. Absolutely!"

26

A Worm in the Apple

I was feeling cranky when López arrived this afternoon, and not even entirely sure why. Superficially it was because I had bought some peaches only yesterday from the supermarket, and when I went to the bowl today to treat myself, I found that one of them was already rotten. I was just in the process of removing it from the bowl when he appeared in the doorway.

"You don't look too happy today," he said. I told him about my fruit frustrations, leaving him in no doubt about my opinion.

"Strong feelings," he remarked. "I wonder what that is really about."

"Don't put your spiritual director's hat on with me," I said, rather more vehemently than I intended.

"All right, calm down," he said. "It's only a peach. Or, is it?"

"I chose them really carefully," I said. "They looked so good, but if I don't get rid of this rotten one, it will infect the whole lot."

He left me in the silence for a while until I began to see for myself that this was about more than peaches.

I found myself telling him about how disillusioned I was feeling, with one person in particular who had seemed so "spiritual" and yet had acted quite treacherously.

"You expect people in spirituality circles to be more principled," I complained. "I don't know what to do about it. I am very fearful of confrontation."

"One little worm can rot the whole apple," he said. "It nearly happened to us."

When I had calmed myself enough to sit and listen, he went on to tell me about some of his impressions along the rocky roads of Rome.

"I arrived in the Eternal City with my own high expectations," he said, "even though Jerusalem was really where I wanted to be. Since that was proving to be impossible, we had freely offered our services to the pope, as head of the church. I know, of course, that the church is a human organization and inevitably flawed, but I wasn't prepared for the level of corruption I found in Rome, or for the huge discrepancy between the magnificent churches and palaces and the inadequate housing where the poor people had to live. *Where is Jesus in this?* I asked myself.

"I hadn't felt easy about Rome all along, as I mentioned. I had a kind of premonition of problems ahead. You sensed that, I think, when I told you about my fears on that narrow cliff path outside Bologna."

I nodded in confirmation. "I guess it takes only a few worms to turn the Eternal City into an infernal city," I said.

"At first, everything went smoothly. We were well received, and supported by benefactors. We were even given a small house to live in and supplies of food. We tried to live simply, sleeping on the floor and passing most of the food on to people in greater need than we were. We were trying to follow Jesus in a city and a system that seemed in many ways to be heading in the opposite direction."

I wondered to myself how much had actually changed in that respect, through the intervening centuries, but I kept quiet.

"Maybe our example did some good," he went on, "because quite a few people asked to make the *Exercises*. Even Dr. Ortiz, who had once denounced me to the Inquisition. He became a fervent supporter. I remember him saying that the *Exercises* offered a way of discovering not 'what to believe' but rather 'how to live,' and when I heard that, I knew we must be getting something right.

"But then the storm broke. There was a malicious anonymous campaign against us centered in the Curia, the papal administration, accusing us of being dishonest and nonorthodox. I was even accused of being a heretic on the run, a Lutheran in disguise! The old story really, but this time the source of it all was one of 'ours'! A man called Landivar had been with us for quite a while and knew a lot about us—knew where to hit us where we were vulnerable. He had left the society and felt slighted in some way, so this was his revenge."

"How dreadful, to be attacked in such an underhand way by someone you had trusted," I said. "What did you do?"

"I did what you have just done when you threw out the rotten peach. I identified the source of the problem and confronted it. I asked for a meeting with Pope Paul III and talked things through with him directly. I asked for a fair trial, by any judge the pope might nominate. If found guilty, I would take the punishment. If not, I would expect a formal, written declaration of our innocence."

"What happened?" I asked.

"We were vindicated. Our accusers were later charged with heresy themselves, and the companions were completely exonerated."

"It took courage to confront things so directly," I said.

"It does take courage, and it entails risk," he said, "but it's the only way. It's the way of truth. And truth will set you free, eventually."

He paused for a moment while I reflected on what to do about the "Landivar" in my own life.

"The secret is to notice when, and how, the destructive spirit is at work and then confront that spirit before it undermines all the work of the creative spirit. No use prevaricating and compromising and trying to appease the destructive spirit, or tiptoe around it. You have to act against it. You can always tell when a destructive spirit is abroad. It spreads an atmosphere of unease and fear and disquiet. It leaves a bad smell in its wake. That's a sure sign that it's time to act against it. But remember that it isn't the actual *person* who is the problem but the destructive spirit that is acting through that person."

"Thanks," I said. "That's really very helpful."

"Feeling a bit brighter now?" he asked.

"Just a bit."

"Let me lift those spirits for you." He grinned. And then, to my complete amazement, he started to dance!

He performed a fantastic Basque dance, right there in my apartment, just for me. I felt my depression lifting and a lighthearted joy returning. By the time he had finished his performance, we were both laughing.

"I did that once for someone who was making the *Exercises* and got a bit low," he said. "It's not something I am in the habit of doing, but, after all, we do both follow the Lord of the Dance."

27

The Reluctant General

It was a rare and lovely summer's afternoon. A gentle breeze mellowed the sun's heat. In the hedge, the wild roses were blooming, and their scent awoke a memory in my heart of how often as a child I had stretched out on the grass with a book and drifted off to a world of dreams, carried on the scent of wild roses in the garden of my childhood home before the family conflicts over my brother began.

I glanced across to my companion, sitting at my little garden table. He was busily writing in his notebook. The script was immaculate. I was ashamed of my own scrawl, which was probably why I had migrated to the laptop to carry on my own correspondence.

"What's brewing in that notebook, López?" I asked gently, as I deposited a fresh glass of lemonade at his side.

He smiled and laid down his pen for a while, apparently welcoming this respite from his labor.

"It isn't easy," he admitted, "to organize a whole company of people from many different backgrounds and cultures and with such widely varying temperaments and expectations."

"I can well believe it," I said, wondering how it might feel for this man of action, this inveterate pilgrim, this restless searcher, to find himself tied to a desk and a mountain of administrative tasks as he strove to shape his companions into a coherent organization that would hold together through the centuries that lay ahead.

"More and more people are joining our little group," he said. "So we need to be clear about where we are going and what is the best route to follow in these times of such extreme upheaval. Every question I address seems to bring a dozen more in its wake. I think it may take me a lifetime to work it all out, but

I'm not in any great hurry. I will just keep at it for as long as it takes."

"Your wisdom would be very helpful to us as we struggle with all the upheavals of life here in the twenty-first century," I said, hoping that he might drop a few hints from the labor of love he was engaged in.

I wasn't disappointed. He sat back and surveyed his notes, then turned to me, glad, perhaps, to have an opportunity to review his own thoughts out loud.

"First you have to be clear about what your ideals and intentions are," he said. "A whole new world is opening up for us in our turbulent times. This brings challenges and opportunities that none of us has ever considered, or even imagined. Committing ourselves to serving God wherever we are needed is a risky thing to do. We could get sent just about anywhere. We could be pitched into situations and dangers no one can predict. So it's very important to stay tuned in to the signs of the times, to let life teach us as we go, to be open to all possibilities, yet also discerning about which paths are good to follow and which are not.

"It seems to me that as a general rule we should engage with those challenges that are more likely to draw people to God, or where there is the most need, and the hope of the greater harvest. The question might be, Which fields of action are more likely to add to humanity's store of love, hope, and trust? And then, of course, it's about finding the people most suited to carry out particular tasks."

"So you are into Human Resources as well as Strategic Planning?" I smiled.

"I suppose so. And we also need to ensure good leadership," he added, "and that is going to be a problem."

I would have thought, personally, that it was obvious who should lead this fledgling society—surely López himself, its founder and inspiration.

"I'm trying to set down what it takes to be a good leader," he said.

I thought of how desperately our world today needs good leaders and what a monumental lack of them there is.

"And what qualities would *you* look for in a leader?" I asked him.

"Someone who walks close to God. A prayerful person. One who has vision and can set other people's hearts on fire. Someone who is master of himself but a servant of others. A humble person. Someone who knows his own weakness and is therefore tolerant of the weakness of others. A person of courage who won't be deflected from a true course by the threat of danger or opposition, or compromise his integrity to gain wealth or status or power. A person who can persevere doggedly when the going is difficult. A person who can hold tensions in a creative balance. A person who knows what a mess he is and is willing to let the Spirit hover over his chaos and bring about a new creation."

"Wow!" I exclaimed. "You're not asking for much, are you?"

He looked suddenly embarrassed.

"We do this democratically," he said. "We held a secret ballot."

"And?"

"They elected *me*!"

"Congratulations," I said. "You were the obvious choice."

"Not at all," he said, with the quirk of an eyebrow. "I insisted that they all pray about it and vote again."

"And the result?"

"Me again," he muttered rather crossly. "I refused, of course. I'm absolutely not the one to lead them."

I thought back to the ambitious soldier I had first encountered and how, in his youth, he would have done anything to achieve the rank of general. And now, as it was being urged upon him in a very different context, he was resolutely rejecting it.

"So what happens now?" I asked.

"In desperation I brought the whole matter to my confessor," he said, "and reminded him of how utterly unworthy my life has been, and how it would be pre-posterous for me to become the general of this new Society."

"What did he say?"

"He told me that if I keep on rejecting the unan-imous choice of the companions, I could actually be resisting the Holy Spirit. He told me in no uncertain terms that I should accept."

With this, the newly elected, reluctant first superior general of the Society of Jesus laid aside his pen, drank his chilled lemonade, and bowed his head in prayer.

28

The Power of the Pen

I was just trying to catch up with my emails when the door opened and López came in. I greeted him warmly, glad that he felt sufficiently at home at my place to come and go so freely.

"I'll be right with you," I promised him. "Just sending off a few messages."

"Take your time," he said, and then came up alongside me, gazing in wonderment at my laptop and its remarkable ability to connect me with friends across the world.

"I could have done with something like that in my time," he commented, with a flicker of envy. "That would have made my correspondence load a great deal easier."

"You wrote a lot?" I asked.

"Around seven thousand letters in nine years," he said.

"Good heavens—that's a letter a day!" I was thinking of how hard I find it just to keep up with a few emails.

"Here," I offered, "try the laptop. Just for the experience!"

He took up the invitation eagerly, and I left him typing away while I went to fix the coffee.

"Here, have a look," he said, when I returned. "This will give you an idea of the kind of letters I wrote, how I tried to keep in touch with old friends, give advice and confront wrongdoing, and, above all, to stay connected to 'ours' when sometimes they were very far away."

"Are you sure this isn't private?" I asked.

"I think you'll find they are all published now," he replied resignedly. Nothing stays private forever.

He flicked through the neatly arranged folders he had managed to set up on my laptop database and brought up a few samples to show me. He had plenty to say about the question of obedience, for example.

"I guess that must always be a big thing for people living in community," I said.

"When a person takes a vow of obedience, he is actually agreeing to the belief that his superior is God's representative and must be obeyed as if the instruction came from God directly."

"That's a big leap of faith, isn't it," I said, not trying to hide my lack of confidence in such a system.

"I suppose it must look like that to you, nowadays," he said. "Back then it was accepted that the church was the Bride of Christ and received her authority from God himself. Look at this letter here, for example." He brought up a long epistle to his companions in Portugal, written in 1553, in which he read them the riot act about precisely why they should do as he had instructed them and stop trying to do things their own way. This was no request; it was very definitely a command. Written in the language of a wise counsellor and father figure, it was nevertheless the old soldier who was wielding the pen.

"You had a number of female friends and correspondents, didn't you?"

"Very good friends, and benefactors too. I owe a very great deal to the women in my life."

"But you didn't want them in your society?" I pressed him.

He paused to compose his thoughts it seemed, then told me that there had been, indeed, a handful of female companions.

"My old friend and supporter Isabel Roser was very determined to become one of the companions. She was so determined that she wrote to the pope directly and asked permission for herself; her lady-in-waiting, Francisca Cruyllas; and her friend Lucrezia di Brodine, to take vows and become companions along with me. You could say she forced my hand. I could hardly argue with the pope. They all made their vows to me on Christmas Day, 1545."

"And did it work out?"

"Let's just say they didn't get through the novitiate. They weren't suited for communal life. I always believed women were better led in these things by other women and not by men. It all became very embarrassing, and Isabel was furious when I had to ask the pope to rescind his permission."

"Hmm," I murmured. "And yet now there must be hundreds of thousands of women who are walking the path you mapped out."

"That's true." He looked at me brightly. "And that delights me beyond measure. With hindsight, maybe I was a bit hasty in ruling it out." At this he cast me a sideways smile. "Things change," he went on. "But there was one lady who remained one of 'ours' until her death. That was no less a person than Princess Juana of Spain, daughter of the emperor Charles V. She took vows after being widowed shortly after her marriage. Well, it's hard to say no to the highest lady in the land. She stayed with us all her life."

He closed the folder containing the letters to his many female friends. "I thank God sincerely for these friendships, even though some of them got a bit stormy." He sighed.

"But letters must have been a crucial method of staying in touch with your companions when you were dispersed around the world."

"Oh, definitely," he said, clicking open a huge folder containing letters to his brothers all over Europe and beyond, encouraging them, instructing them, warning them of dangers and pitfalls, and explaining his reasons for various decisions that affected them. Some were to whole groups of them, some to individuals.

Some would end with the simple "Poor in goodness" or "The poor pilgrim." Others concluded more tersely, but all were remarkable for the detail with which the writer addressed particular situations or concerns.

He smiled as he closed down the laptop and stretched out his hand for the coffee I was offering. His voluminous correspondence made my emails look like notes passed between schoolchildren. But at least, I consoled myself, nobody was ever likely to publish my limp efforts to stay in touch. López had written with serious intention and for a world that seemed solid and permanent, where his advice had an almost eternal quality. Now we live in a world where everything is in flux and nothing is forever. Our Internet exchanges are just ripples on the surface of a shifting ocean.

"It's a great little device," he commented. "But some things are worth putting into real letters."

29

Futures

Since López seemed to be remarkably comfortable with the challenges of modern technology, I decided to risk something that I thought might interest him. It was a while before he dropped by again. I sensed that his health was failing and he was getting tired. The relentless demands of his administrative role were probably getting him down, there in his small room in Rome, even though, characteristically, he was responding to them with unstinting energy.

It occurred to me that he might be able to use an injection of hope and inspiration, and I figured I could help by offering him a glimpse into the crystal ball of the centuries ahead of him.

"Sit down and make yourself comfortable," I invited him, when he finally materialized again. He seemed grateful for the chance to take the weight off his feet and sank into his favorite chair without waiting for a second bidding. Once he was settled, I dialed up the Skype link on my computer and invited him to meet a few of his sons and daughters at work. And one by one they appeared on the screen to meet their founding father.

I should have been used to being surprised by López by now. Surprise had been the hallmark of our entire relationship. But tonight I was truly amazed to see his eyes light up with pure joy—and a degree of admissible pride—as he watched the images flicker across the screen. We began by watching clips of various scenes around the world.

A Jesuit retreat center in the UK was featured in a TV documentary in which we watched a random group of very ordinary people being gently, skillfully, and sometimes challengingly guided through the *Exercises*. And then the landslide of requests from others who had seen the TV program and now wanted to come and try making a retreat themselves.

The scene switched to El Salvador, where the local people were grieving for their heroes, a group of Jesuits and their coworkers who had been murdered by the militia for daring to stand up for the poorest of the people and speak the values of the Gospel into the corruption and violence of the ruling regime.

In Hong Kong we dropped into a meeting of the Jesuits and lay partners working across Australasia and gathered on Cheung Chau Island to share their experience. I noticed how López winced when we heard of the valiant attempts of lay partners in Malaysia to keep their vision alive in spite of fierce opposition from both the government and the church. I could see that this was bringing López's own experience of ecclesiastical resistance to mind, and I felt his prayers winging across the South China Sea to these beleaguered sons and daughters.

But tears of deep consolation streamed across his face as a young nun, who had managed to establish a retreat center in mainland China in spite of significant obstacles, told us in tones of quiet conviction and gentle humility that she believed the *Spiritual Exercises* had the potential to transform her country. And he smiled broadly when he learned that his dear friend Francis Xavier had passed close by this very coast on his journey to Japan. But a shadow clouded his brow for a brief moment as he reflected. "I never saw him again after he set out on that journey."

In South Africa, another young girl tugged at his heart as she told us that she was enthusiastically adapting the *Exercises* for an African worldview. "Fantastic!" he murmured, as he listened to her sharing of her experience during childhood of resistance to the apartheid regime in which she had grown up, and how she had turned this experience into the kind of wisdom that could set other peoples' hearts alight, inspired by the wisdom of the *Exercises*.

The screen flickered again as we watched sisters and lay supporters in the United States valiantly supporting efforts to establish just and equitable health care for the millions of marginalized in the world's richest economy. "We are working for a faith that does justice," they proclaimed, "even though this brings us into conflict with many of our fellow citizens." I heard López sigh deeply. "Love shows itself in action," he said.

In a tiny room in a big house in North Wales, a young Jesuit with intense features was writing poetry. He had suppressed his muse for many years in an effort to live only for God, until he discovered that God is in all things, including in his own precious gift of poetry. And the voice of Gerard Manley Hopkins rang out across the room:

All things therefore are charged with love, are charged with God and if we know how to touch them give off sparks and take fire, yield drops and flow, ring and tell of him.

"Thank God he discovered the freedom to write again," López commented.

Australian saint Mary MacKillop, newly beatified, but not before she had been demonized and even excommunicated, greeted López warmly and reminded him that she had found shelter with the Jesuits during her darkest hours. The imperative of the *Exercises* to let love be revealed in action had taken root deep within her.

"*Never see a need without doing something about it*," she said, and López vehemently nodded his affirmation.

The scene changed to a quiet graveyard in a hidden corner of upstate New York, where daffodils flourished on the grave of Jesuit paleontologist Pierre Teilhard de Chardin, who had shocked his contemporaries and earned himself an ecclesiastical ban by suggesting that the human family is evolving into a state of consciousness, an Omega point, that could fully reflect the image of God, if we have the courage to embrace its call. We could hear his voice rising up from the fertile earth in which he lay:

Someday, after mastering the winds, the waves, the tides and gravity, we shall harness for God the energies of love, and then, for a second time in the history of the world, we will have discovered fire.

"He reminds me of Martin in the smithy back at Loyola," López remarked. "He knows that a spark of the divine love in a human heart can set the world on fire and transform the future."

A Yorkshire woman, Mary Ward, was the inspiration for our next guests—groups of sisters and lay partners around the world who had committed themselves to be a presence of Christ in the world and not the cloisters, just as López had done.

"These are your sisters and daughters," I reminded him, "and I hope you will welcome them. Mary Ward discovered God's call in times of grave religious persecution in seventeenth-century England. She, too, was suppressed by the pope of her time, charged with heresy, and imprisoned by the Inquisition. For her, too, gold had been forged in the crucible of suffering."

"I welcome them with wide-open arms and a wide-open heart," he said, his eyes brimming with tears.

And finally came a Spanish Jesuit from López's own country, born in Bilbao, a man called Pedro Arrupe. Arrupe had been medically trained and was in Hiroshima in 1945 when the atomic bomb fell. He shared with us the story of how he had tended the sick and dying there, and how he had gone on to struggle for peace and justice in Latin America, thus incurring the opposition of the Vatican—an opposition that still prevails when liberation theology is mentioned.

"Pedro became the twenty-eighth General of the Jesuits," I whispered to López, though I'm sure he didn't need me to tell him this. "And in that role he persuaded your sons to work actively for the promotion of justice, even though it would put their lives in danger. When he had to resign because of poor health, the Vatican tried to impose their own choice of a new General and caused quite a crisis in the ranks. It was Arrupe who steered the society through those troubled times."

"When we encounter opposition, either from church or state," López commented, "then we know we are living true to the gospel of Christ."

But when we asked Arrupe for a final word on our journey through the future, that word wasn't *justice* but *love*, a word that defined this man who totally loved God and totally loved God's people.

"*What you are in love with, what seizes your imagination, will affect everything. Fall in love, stay in love, and it will decide everything,*" he told us.

"Exactly right!" López's face was glowing with the very fire that he, himself, had kindled in millions of human hearts. A fire of courage, passion, vision, commitment, and compassion, being lived out and carried forward in so many different ways all across the world.

"Thank you!" He turned to me as I powered down the computer.

"No," I protested. "It is we who thank *you*."

𝔔 30 𝔔

Two Stories Meet

*B*ecause our previous meeting had ended on such a high note, I didn't really expect to see López again. We had journeyed through his story, nearly to its end, and I sensed a finality to the work we had done—if we could even call it work.

But a mere two days later I walked onto the deck at daybreak after a sleepless night. And there he was, in his chair, apparently enjoying the morning light and the unseasonably mild temperature.

"López—how good to see you! Have you had your morning coffee yet?" I turned to go put on the kettle, but he held up a hand to make me pause.

"I don't need coffee. I need to talk with you." His seriousness pulled me to my chair, and I sat down. We looked at each other, and I waited for him to say more. But moments went by without a sound. Finally I stifled a yawn and said, trying not to sound impatient, "I'm all ears—what do you have to tell me?"

"No, what do you have to tell *me*?" He sat very still, holding me in a concentrated gaze. "All this time I have shared my life with you, even my desperate struggles. And I've known that you were fighting some silent battles of your own. I don't want to leave without knowing what you have decided."

"My work is limping along, and I'm keeping at it. It's my heart's desire, which you've helped me see is also God's desire for me. I'm really grateful to you for that."

"Yes, I know your work will be all right. But what about the other thing?" I looked at him in surprise, and he continued. "Not all the messages on your phone and computer were about your workshops and speaking engagements."

I sighed. My inner turmoil was rising out of control.

"See—when a person sighs like that, and looks so heartbroken, God is speaking." He leaned toward me. "What do you think divine love is saying to you right now?"

"It's a long story, López."

"No longer than mine, I'm sure. Do *you* need coffee?" Before I could answer, he was in my kitchen, heating water and pulling cups and saucers from the cabinet. I was grateful, because that gave me time to gather my thoughts. When he came back with tray in hand, I took my cup and began.

"I mentioned getting a call from my brother—that time I was about to call someone else and speak my mind?"

"I remember. You said he was in a situation of some sort."

"That's putting it mildly. He's been in a 'situation' from his earliest years. Drinking, drugs, trouble with the police—"

"A modern-day version of my younger self, it sounds like."

"Yes, but no conversions for him, at least nothing that lasted. Our parents could never bring themselves to admit he had problems; in fact, they made it easier for him to continue on his path. It was the source of heated arguments between me and them. A lot of hard feelings connected to Ricky." I gulped the coffee to help keep down the lump that was rising in my throat and threatening to choke me. López watched me with gentle eyes.

"At one point, nearly twenty years ago, he was living in my home—with my husband and me. We were trying hard to work at our marriage, which both sets of parents had so disapproved of—my husband was a recent immigrant and experiencing a lot of prejudice. Ricky's presence was making things a lot more difficult. He promised to clean up, and he did all right for a while. We wanted to give him a safe, loving home while he got his life on track. But it wasn't long before all the signs came back—signs that he was in trouble again." I looked at López and took a shaky breath. "I had to put our marriage and our own needs first, and I knew the only chance of bringing Ricky to his senses would be a sharp shock—or 'tough love,' as we call it now. So I told my brother to leave. I forced him out."

The tears refused to be held back anymore. My friend sat quietly while I let them stream down my cheeks. "God only knows what that cost Ricky—being turned out like that. It was the most awful choice I've ever made."

"But do you regret it?"

I shook my head. "As you and I have talked these months, I have reviewed all the reasonings and feelings and circumstances of that situation. I've weighed it all against what we have discovered about discernment. And I do think it was the right choice, just horribly costly. But I've never had what I could call feelings of consolation about this."

"Not all heartbreak is desolation," he said. "Just as not all happiness means we're doing the right thing. Sometimes the only consolation is this sense you have experienced—of knowing this was the right thing to do. God wants you to be free, Rachel. You must let go of the past."

"If there were only the past to think of." I sipped coffee again while he waited to hear more.

"Not long before you and I met, my brother contacted me again. At first I thought he was just wanting help as he has so many times before—a place to stay, money, something like that. We've hardly spoken a dozen words to each other in as many years. But when I finally gave him the chance to speak, he broke my heart."

López handed me a tissue. "What's happened?"

"Well, Ricky's in jail—not for the first time—and he'll be there for a while. That's hardly news anymore. But it turns out he has a little boy. And the mom's no longer in the picture." I looked at López, wanting to see his expression as I continued. "Ricky wants me to take his son, give him a home. The boy's six years old, and I've never laid eyes on him. And I've no idea how to go about raising a child. You see," I said, trembling with suppressed emotion, "my husband and I . . . we could never have children of our own."

López sat back, his eyebrows high, his eyes like great pools of compassion. "This is definitely a new situation."

"And I need to make a decision soon. Ryan has been staying with friends of Ricky's, but it's quite temporary, and social services will step in anytime and move him to some group home or foster family. My emotions are in such turmoil over this, it's hard to think. This would disrupt my work, because since my husband's death, it's just me here."

"You've spent a good deal of time thinking about this."

"Of course—it's on my mind all the time."

"You've attended to your feelings about it."

"Which go back and forth at extremes! What a blessed gift—to be able to give this child a home. And he's family, which makes me even more eager to help. But Ricky's life is not one I want to get tangled in any more than necessary. And caring for a child so young is no little task, especially at my age and on my own. Also, there are wonderful young foster families, many people out there who could be good for Ryan. I don't want to put myself in the way of an even better solution for him."

López was drinking his coffee thoughtfully. "So, you have weighed the pros and cons—which is a good step to take. But not enough to give you an answer."

"I'm afraid not."

"May I suggest another method or two?"

"Please do. Whatever choice I make will have a drastic impact."

"Imagine you're on your death bed," he began.

"Are you serious?!"

"Very serious. Imagine you have only moments left to live. And you're reviewing your life, and this situation comes to memory. Looking back on the whole of your life and at this dilemma, which decision would you like to have made? Which decision would give you more ease, now that you are at death's door?"

"All right." I tried to imagine, but it was difficult with a friend looking on. I saw López smile.

"This might take some time, and it will probably go better when you're alone. Listen to a second idea."

"Go ahead."

"Imagine that this dilemma is not yours but is the situation of someone else. And that person comes to you for counsel. Listen carefully to this friend, notice everything about her while she talks about it—her mood, her expression, all the unspoken clues to what's going on in her soul. Then counsel her as best you can. It may turn out that this is the counsel appropriate for you."

I felt a sense of calm work its way through me. What my friend suggested sounded workable.

"One more thing," he added. "Try letting yourself live for a few days, in your imagination, as though you had definitely made the decision to say no to Ricky. Notice how you feel about it as you live with it like this. Notice whatever movements show up within you. Then do the exercise the other way round. Spend a few days living as though you had made the decision to take Ryan. How does that feel? What inner movements does that choice bring up in you? Live with your two options for as long as you need, weighing them up, without actually taking action either way. And remember to ask for help—to be able to see all of this through

God's eyes," he continued. "In the end, all is grace, you know."

"Thank you, López. Even speaking about this out loud—to a caring friend—has helped me settle down. It's odd how present and focused we can be for other people and yet how confused we can become when the issues get personal."

He got up then, rather abruptly I thought. I noticed then how old he looked, and how weary.

"Trust what God has already taught you, throughout your life," he said. "All your life has prepared you for this decision—I really believe that. It's certainly been the case for me."

Then, "You have some discerning to do," he said. "And I have much correspondence to attend to." He walked down the steps of my deck.

I watched as he continued to the street. His limp appeared to be not a disability but a distinguishing mark of who he was. There he went, unable to walk straight, carrying with him a history of imperfection—and grace.

À-Dieu

He sat calmly and serenely in his favorite chair, which I had now come to regard as "López's place." I quietly contemplated the features of the man who had so unaccountably chosen to share something of himself with me, as these remarkable months had passed. He was deep in thought, his brow furrowed, his expression a curious mixture of sorrow and joy, frustration and fulfillment. Here was a man so very different from the flamboyant young soldier who had once presented himself at my doorway, so different from the tormented soul who had shared with me his struggles at Manresa, so different—and yet so essentially the same. It was as though, as his story had unfolded in the space between us, his true self, the essence of who he truly is, had emerged from a cocoon to fly free, a soul who is at once both deeply and authentically humble and also totally confident of the path he walks and the one who walks it with him and in him, sure-footed in those pilgrim sandals. The God within him had encountered and embraced the God beyond him.

This man had seemed such a total mess. How had he become a mystic? We cannot fathom what goes on within the cocoon to reshape the ego-driven caterpillar that has no other notion of its destiny than to eat up every leaf in sight, including the one it is sitting on, into the magnificence of the butterfly, fluttering freely through creation, enjoying what leads to life, rejecting what is destructive of life, simply being what it is. López's story had given me some small insight into what had been going on within the cocoon of his heart, what had been coming to be in the crucible of his pain and his passion.

A nugget of gold had emerged from that crucible. I knew that this gold had become a currency of transformation for many hundreds of thousands of souls, including my own, who would learn from his wisdom and follow his footsteps in the years that had already intervened since his earthly life and the years that would still unfold. I was profoundly and overwhelmingly grateful that I had been knocked off my bicycle that distant day, and rescued by a stranger, who had chosen to open up something of his story in the conversations we had shared.

Yet the shadow of inevitable parting hung over us this evening.

I looked deeply into his eyes, and I saw a weariness, a worn-out-ness, of one whose path is almost walked and who will soon walk beyond the horizon. I felt my tears rising. I wanted to tell him how grateful I was for all he had given, not just to me but to so many, but the words dissolved formlessly into the silence that held us in its sacred bond.

I walked to the window to gaze at the darkening sky. A single star was rising. I turned to López to draw his attention to it, knowing how much he would love to see it.

But he was gone.

Where he had been sitting there was a little note, written in his beautiful handwriting. I read it through my tears.

Dear friend and companion,

I have not gone far. I have simply gone from Somewhere to Everywhere. Thank you for sharing my story. Trust your own story, for God is in every moment of it. Trust your own experience, for it is the raw material from which God is shaping God's Dream in you. Don't worry that you don't know who or what "God" is. Let the mystery be a mystery, and don't try to grasp it with your own understanding, or pin it down into the limits of your own memory, or manipulate it to conform to your own narrow will. Walk on now in courage, and in deep content. You are God's pilgrim. God's love and grace are all you need.

Thank you, and adieu, my friend,

A poor pilgrim, alongside you,

(Signed:) Íñigo Oñaz López de Loyola

The story is ended and is only just beginning.

He had walked in through my door those many months ago and led me out through his.

The path that lay ahead would reveal itself. Of that I had no doubt.

In Gratitude

This book owes so much to so many, and these words of thanks will fall far short of the gratitude I wish to express.

Above all, it owes its very existence to López himself, who, if you will forgive the temerity of the suggestion, has been a close companion to me throughout the adventure of writing this book. I look forward to continuing these conversations with him in heaven, and hope that he will be merciful toward me in light of my faltering attempts to enter his life, mind, and heart.

Others have companioned this journey also. I thank especially Joe Durepos of Loyola Press, who persuaded me to undertake the task and has encouraged me all along the way, not least by providing a wealth of background reading and regular, affirming e-mails. Also at Loyola Press, I thank Terry Locke, Paul

Campbell, Tom McGrath, and Steve Connor, who are not only invaluable colleagues, but whom I am also privileged to call friends.

My gratitude to Vinita Wright cannot be adequately expressed. I have known Vinita now for several years, as an excellent editor, a very gifted writer, and a much-valued friend. She brought her skills as a novelist to the treatment of Rachel, the narrator, and helped me flesh out that imagined life. Rachel's story not only adds the dimension of a contemporary human experience to the story of López but also provides a wonderful opportunity to illustrate what skillful spiritual direction looks like in practice. So I thank Vinita, not only for her sensitive editing, but also for what she has added to the presence of the narrator.

May I also thank those friends who have been kind enough to read early drafts of the book and share their comments with me—in particular Jane Besly, Wayne Brabin, Norene Costa, Gerard Hughes, Joan Jennings, Bernadette Miles, and Enid Nussbaum. Norene, especially, has journeyed closely, section by section, with López and me. Thank you, Norene, for all your encouragement. I hope López will remain your companion through all the coming years.

Finally, my heartfelt thanks to the sons—and daughters—of Ignatius, who continue to live out their lives in his spirit today and have given me far more than I can ever acknowledge. Thank you very specially to Brian McClorry, who first introduced me to Ignatius and has guided my path with wisdom and friendship ever since, and to Gerry Hughes, dear friend and mentor, who accompanied me through the journey of the *Exercises* and continues to walk alongside me now.

Most of the book was written on my laptop while I was traveling in Australia, and I would like also to thank the Jesuits and lay colleagues in the Australian Province for their inspiration and support, with special greetings to Ian Cribb and the community at Sevenhill in South Australia, where López discovers a new La Storta; also to my friends at the Campion, Canisius, Faber, and Loyola Centres of Ignatian Spirituality in Melbourne, Sydney, Brisbane, and Adelaide respectively.

I am writing these final additions to the book at the Jesuit Retreat Centre on Cheung Chau Island, in the South China Sea, a half-hour ferry ride from Hong Kong Island. Francis Xavier sailed past this island on his way to Japan, and here I have experienced a new and deeply inspiring dimension of the Ignatian Way, through the lens of Asian spirituality, and I have met with other Ignatian pilgrims from the Asia Pacific region. Thank you to Stephen Tong and all the community, friends, and associates of Xavier House and to all friends in the Ignatian Centres in Hong Kong, Malaysia, Singapore, and the Philippines.

To all of you I offer my warmest thanks, and, I am convinced, López sends his greetings and his love.

Suggestions for Further Reading

Bangert, William V. *A History of the Society of Jesus*. St. Louis, MO: Institute of Jesuit Sources, 1999.

Barry, William A. and Robert G. Doherty. *Contemplatives in Action: The Jesuit Way*. New York: Paulist Press, 2002.

Broderick, James. *The Origin of the Jesuits*. Chicago: Loyola Press, 1997.

Broderick, James. *Saint Ignatius Loyola, The Pilgrim Years*. San Francisco: Ignatius Press, 1998.

Derleth, August. *Saint Ignatius and the Company of Jesus*. San Francisco: Ignatius Press, 1999.

Egan, Harvey D. *Ignatius Loyola the Mystic*. Collegeville, MN: Liturgical Press, 1991.

Grogan, Brian. *Alone and On Foot: Ignatius of Loyola*. Dublin: Veritas, 2008.

Kolvenbach, Peter H. *Men of God, Men for Others*. New York: Hyperion, 1999.

Munitiz, Joseph A., and Philip Endean. *Saint Ignatius, Personal Writings*. New York: Penguin Books, 1996.

O'Hara, Tom, and Lynne Muir. *The Gift of Ignatius of Loyola*. Mulgrave, Vic.: John Garratt Publishing, 1999.

O'Malley, John W. *The First Jesuits*. Boston: Harvard University Press, 1995.

Purcell, Mary. *The First Jesuit*. Westminster, MD: Newman Press, 1957.

Rahner, Karl, and Paul Imhof. *Ignatius Loyola*. London: Collins, 1979.

Tellechea Idigoras, Jos Ignacio, (transl. Michael Buckley). *Ignatius of Loyola: The Pilgrim Saint*. Chicago: Loyola University Press, 1994.

Traub, George W. *An Ignatian Spirituality Reader*. Chicago: Loyola Press, 2008.

Tylenda, Joseph N. *A Pilgrim's Journey: The Autobiography of Ignatius of Loyola*. San Francisco: Ignatius Press, 2001.

Young, William J., trans. *St. Ignatius's Own Story, as told to Luis Gonzalez de Camara*. Chicago: Loyola Press, 1998.

Also by Margaret Silf

Simple Faith
Moving Beyond Religion as You Know It
to Grow in Your Relationship with God
$9.95 • Pb • 3623-5 • Also available as an eBook

The Other Side of Chaos
Breaking Through When Life
Is Breaking Down
$13.95 • Pb • 3308-1• Also available as an eBook

Inner Compass
An Invitation to Ignatian Spirituality
$14.95 • Pb • 2645-8 • Also available as an eBook

Close to the Heart
A Guide to Personal Prayer
$12.95 • Pb • 1651-0

Compass Points
Meeting God Every Day at Every Turn
$13.95 • Pb • 2810-0 • Also available as an eBook

To order: call 800-621-1008, visit www.loyolapress.com/store,
or visit your local bookseller.

Continue the Conversation

If you enjoyed this book, then connect with Loyola Press to continue the conversation, engage with other readers, and find out about new and upcoming books from your favorite spiritual writers.

Visit us at
www.LoyolaPress.com
to create an account
and register for our
newsletters.

Or you can just click on the code to the right with your smartphone to sign up.

Connect with us on the following:

You Tube

Facebook
facebook.com/loyolapress

Twitter
twitter.com/loyolapress

You Tube
youtube.com/loyolapress

Continue your Ignatian spirituality journey online …

www.ignatianspirituality.com

Visit us online to

- Join our *E-Magis* newsletter
- Pray the Daily Examen
- Make an online retreat with the *Ignatian Prayer Adventure*
- Participate in the conversation with the dotMagis blog and at facebook.com/ignatianspirituality

1491: Birth
Born Ignacio López de Loyola. He went by Ignatius when living in Rome years later.

1509: Soldier
Ignatius becomes a soldier for the Viceroy of Navarre.

1521: Recovery
Thought to be on his deathbed, Ignatius receives last rites. For the next several months he recovers from his injuries while reading about Jesus Christ and the saints.

1523: Pilgrimage
He embarks on a pilgrimage to the Holy Land.

1523: Jerusalem
He arrives at Jerusalem but due to the political situation at the time, he stays not quite a month and has to return to Spain.

1500   1525   1550

1521: Pamplona
Battle against the French at the fortress of Pamplona; Ignatius is severely injured by a cannonball. The French carry him, on a rough two-week journey, back to the family castle to recover.

1522: Leaves Home
Leaves the Castle Loyola on a mule and heads for the mountain abbey of the Benedictines.

1522: Montserrat
Ignatius arrives at the shrine of Our Lady of Montserrat, where he makes confession, gives his clothing to the poor, leaves his sword and dagger at the altar, and spends the night there in prayer.

1522: Manresa
In Manresa, Ignatius meets Inez Pascual, who shows him a cave near the river Cardoner in which he can stay and pray. He is there several months and begins taking notes that will become the Spiritual Exercises.

1524–1527: Barcelona
Ignatius studies in Barcelona, then at the University of Alcala, then the University of Salamanca.

1528: Paris
He arrives in Paris to study.